75 *Funny* DRAWING PROMPTS WITH OPTIONS

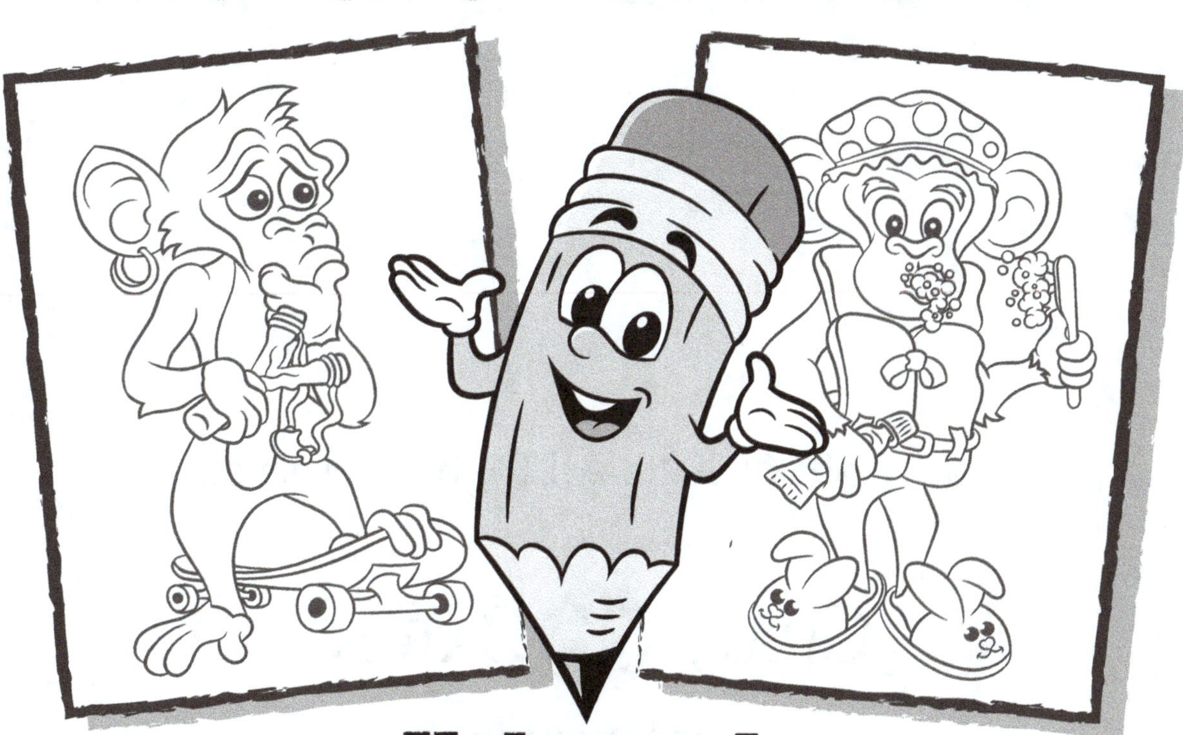

Volume 1

If you would like to see more of my activity book creations, visit my book store at:

CraigBabinBooks.com

ISBN: 978-0-9811446-2-7

This book belongs to:

....

This book was designed to recreate the experience of illustrating for a client. Use the character title of the prompt as the focal point of your drawing. The task is simply there to give you a better idea of the desired traits the character should possess and the objects are to be used to help develop the overall scene. I've drawn two examples of Prompt 1 on the cover of this book to help get you started.

Enjoy!

PROMPT 1

Manic Monkey

The Task: Draw a monkey that looks like it has eaten one too many bananas and is on the verge of becoming emotionally unstable.

Required Objects:

Incorporate at least three of the following items into your drawing. *(See cover for examples)*

Bathing Cap	Flotation Device	Hooped Earrings
Toothbrush	Nasal Spray	Bunny Slippers
Skate Board	Piggy Bank	Bananas
Boxing Gloves	Balloons	Slingshot
Oven Mitts	Mailbox	Binoculars

Manic Monkey

PROMPT 2

Funky Frog

The Task: Draw a frog that is getting its groove on listening to a little uptown funk.

Required Objects:

Incorporate at least three of the following items into your drawing.

Headphones	Sidewalk	Wing Tip Shoes
Fedora	Pimp Coat	Sunglasses
Gold Chains	Bass Guitar	Speakers
Vinyl Record	Fire Hydrant	Cadillac
Cane	Cuff Links	iPod

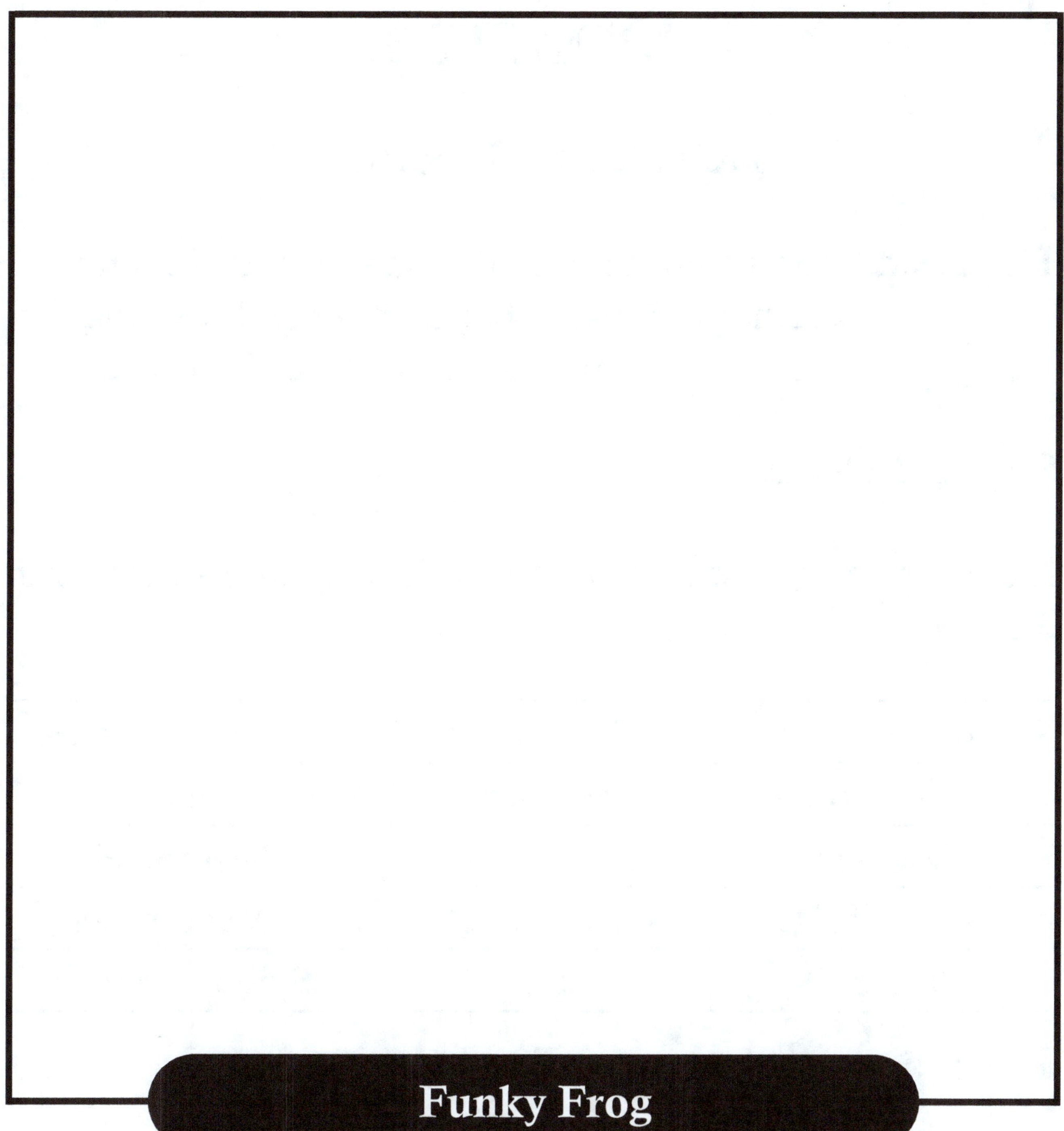

Funky Frog

PROMPT 3

Delusional Dragonfly

The Task: Draw a dragonfly that is so out of touch it actually thinks it has a chance of landing the role of dragon on Game of Thrones.

Required Objects:

Incorporate at least three of the following items into your drawing.

Big Screen TV	Movie Poster	Fire Extinguisher
Toy Sword	Lego Blocks	Lighter
Hair Spray	Shackle & Chains	Plastic Shield
Carton of Eggs	Rejection Letter	DVD Box Set
Old Books	Flag	Suit of Armour

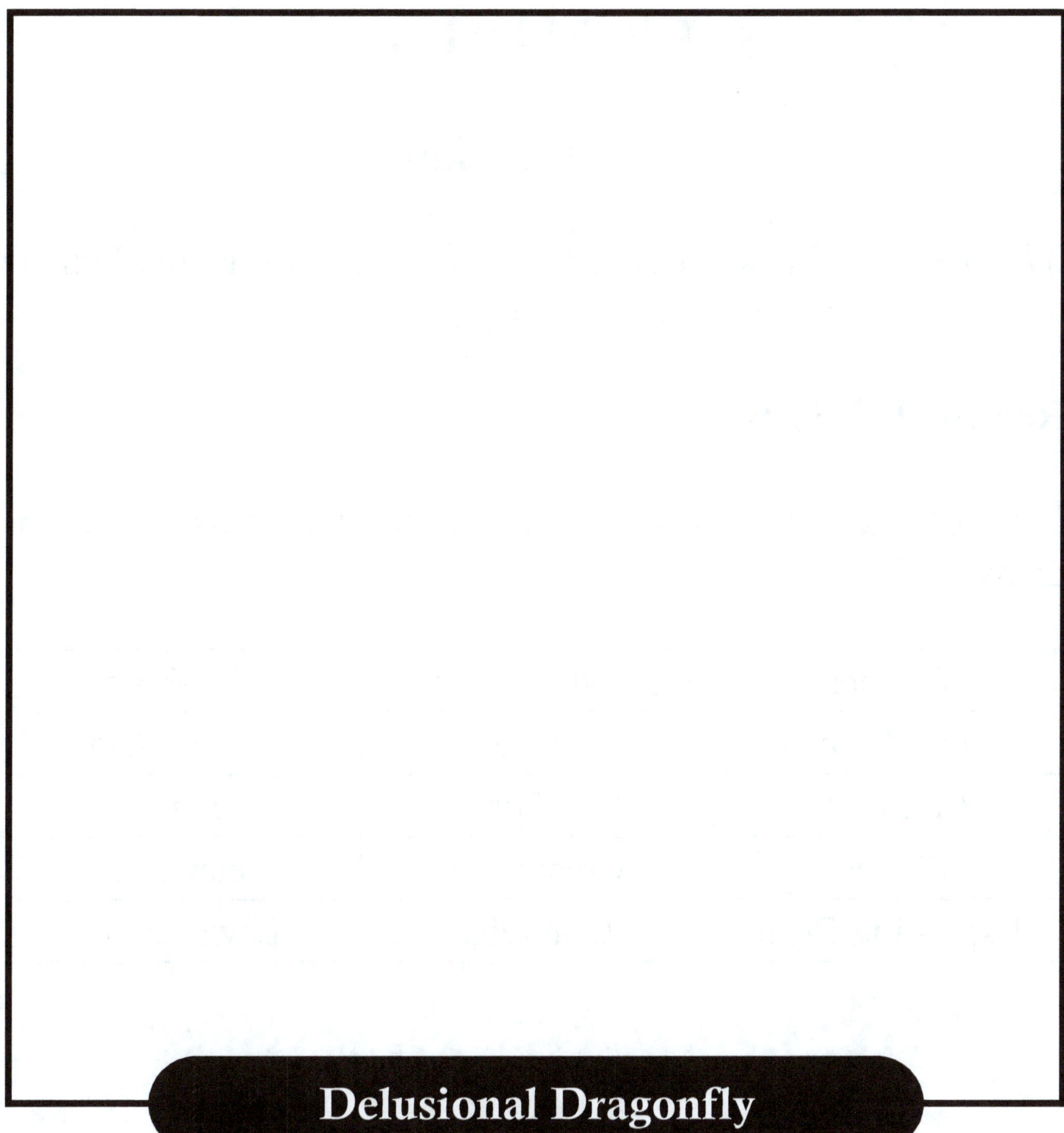

Delusional Dragonfly

PROMPT 4

Laughing Llama

The Task: Draw a llama that looks like it has just heard the funniest joke ever.

Required Objects:

Incorporate at least three of the following items into your drawing.

Feather	First Aid Kit	Big Shoes
Bicycle Horn	Flower	Clown Wig
Rum Bottle	Fart Spray	Tears
Plunger	Cream Pie	Television
Exploding Cigar	Umbrella	Lawn Darts

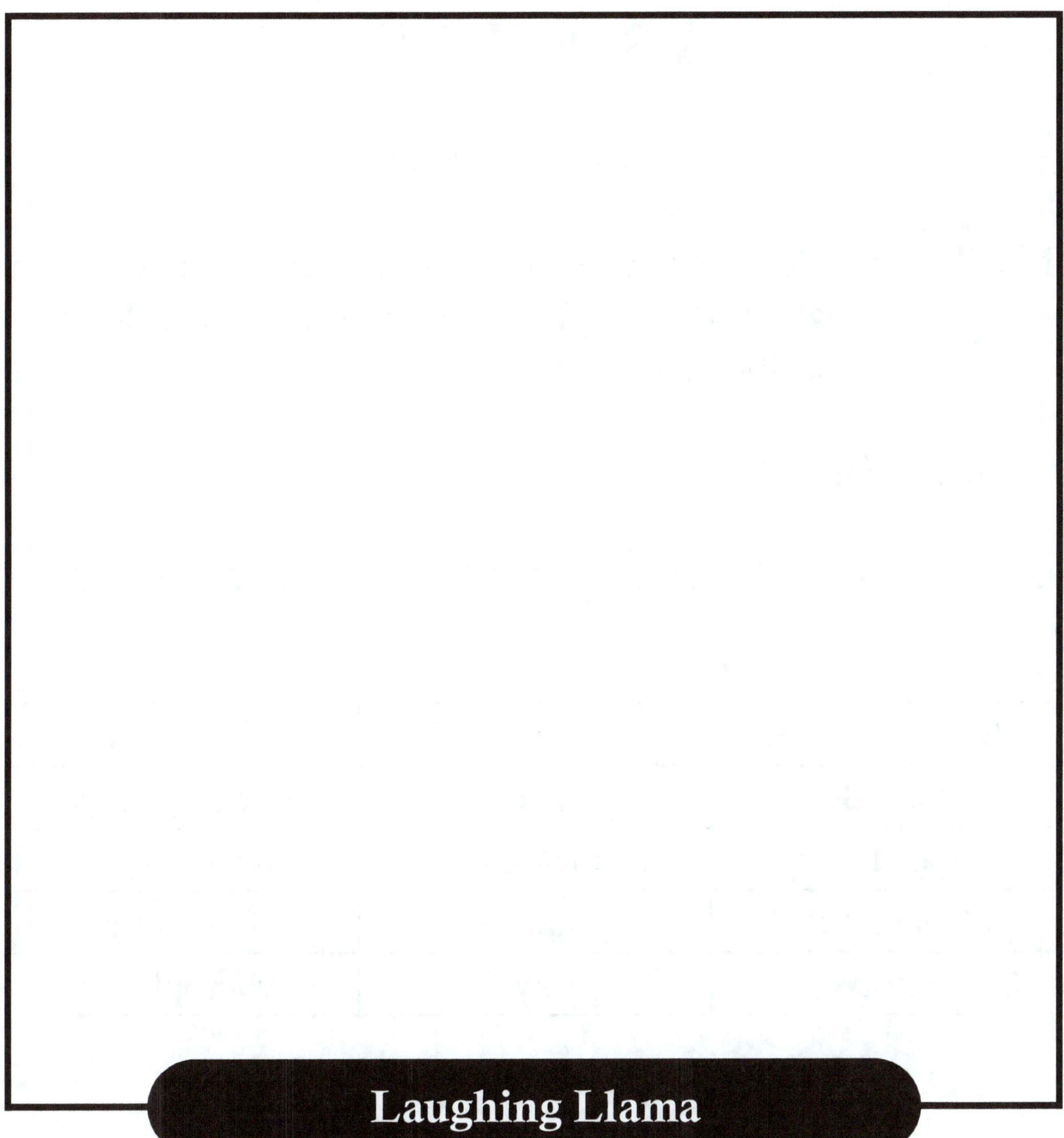
Laughing Llama

PROMPT 5

Boxing Badger

The Task: Draw a badger that looks like it is ready to get in the ring and go toe to toe with Rocky Balboa himself.

Required Objects:

Incorporate at least three of the following items into your drawing.

Boxing Gloves	Title Belt	Sneakers
Teddy Bear	Mirror	Skipping Rope
Speed Bag	Mohawk Hair	School Bell
Wooden Stool	Bucket	Bandages
Shorts	Towel	Microphone

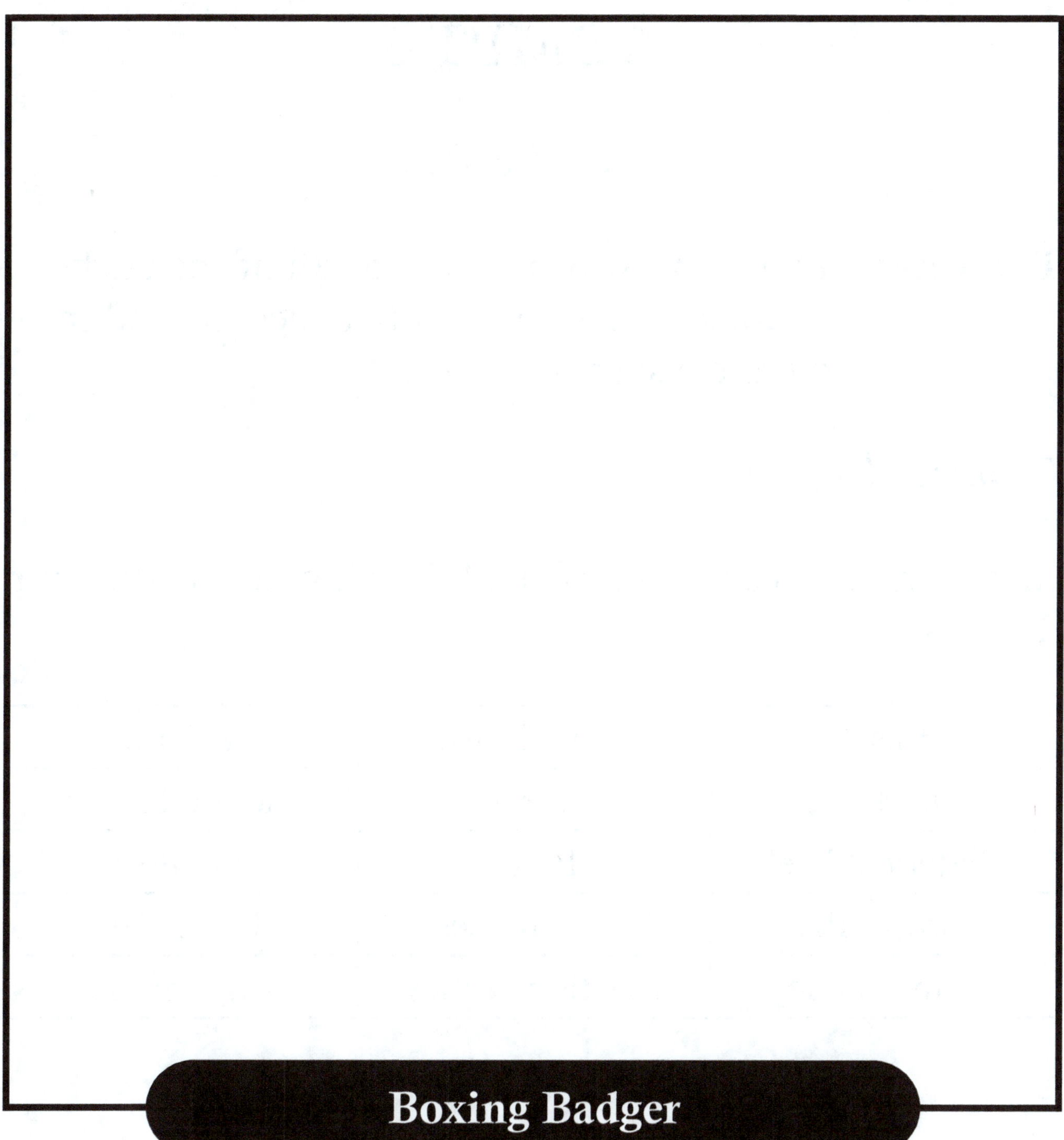

Boxing Badger

PROMPT 6

Artistic Aardvark

The Task: Draw an aardvark that has all of the cliche characteristics you would expect to find in a typical starving artist.

Required Objects:

Incorporate at least three of the following items into your drawing.

Easel	Paint Brush	Palette
Ink Bottle	Overalls	Picture Frame
Pottery Wheel	Beret	Goatee
Flower Pot	Eye Glasses	Paint Can
Wine Bottle	Eviction Notice	Big Thumb

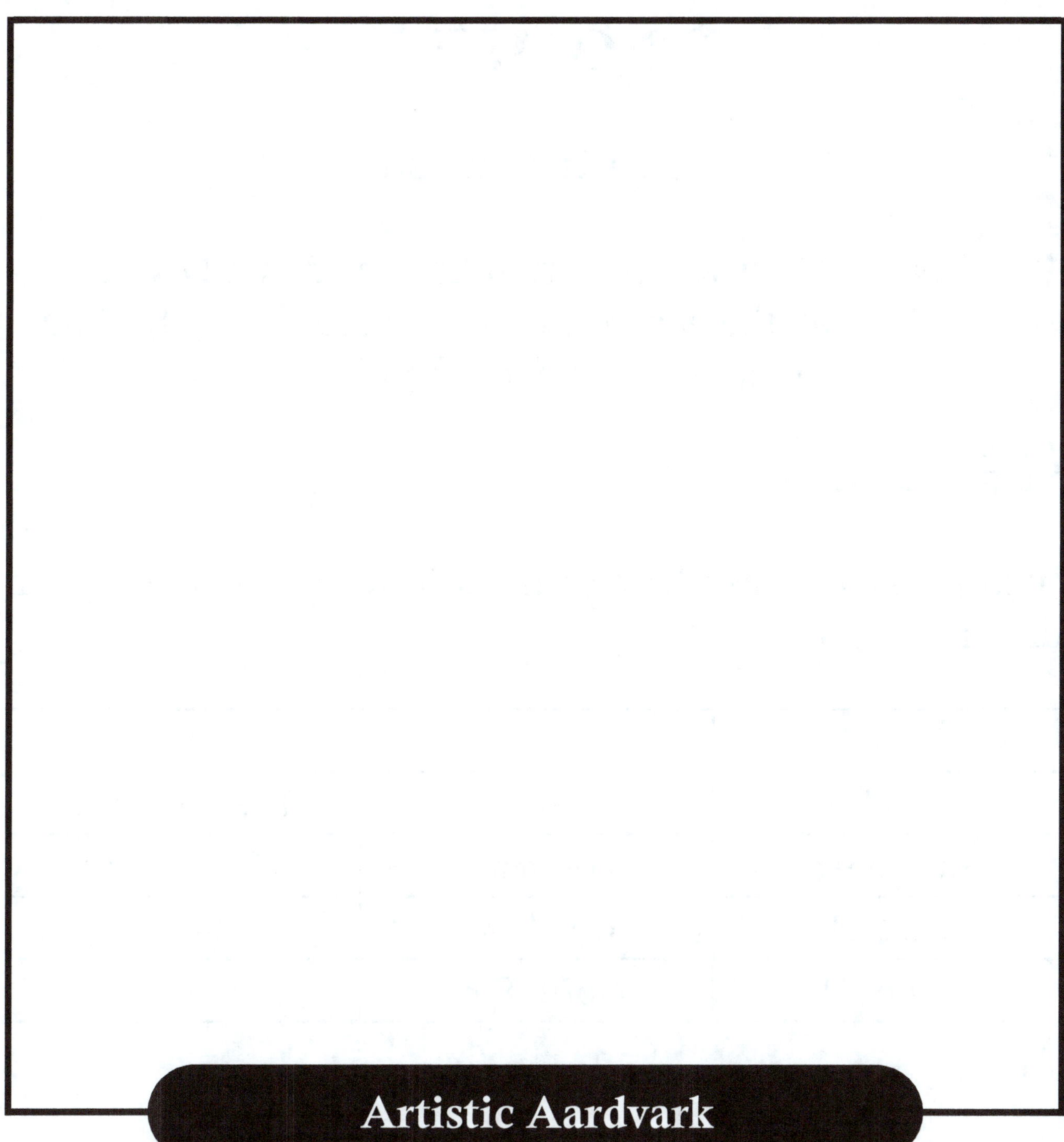
Artistic Aardvark

PROMPT 7

Chillin Catfish

The Task: Draw a catfish that has accidentally swam all the way to the Arctic and is now finding the water a little too frigid.

Required Objects:

Incorporate at least three of the following items into your drawing.

Scarf	Toque	Bonfire
Blanket	Iceberg	Thermometer
Snowboard	Mittens	Coffee Mug
Ice Pick	Ice Skates	Igloo
Aviator Hat	North Pole	Ear Muffs

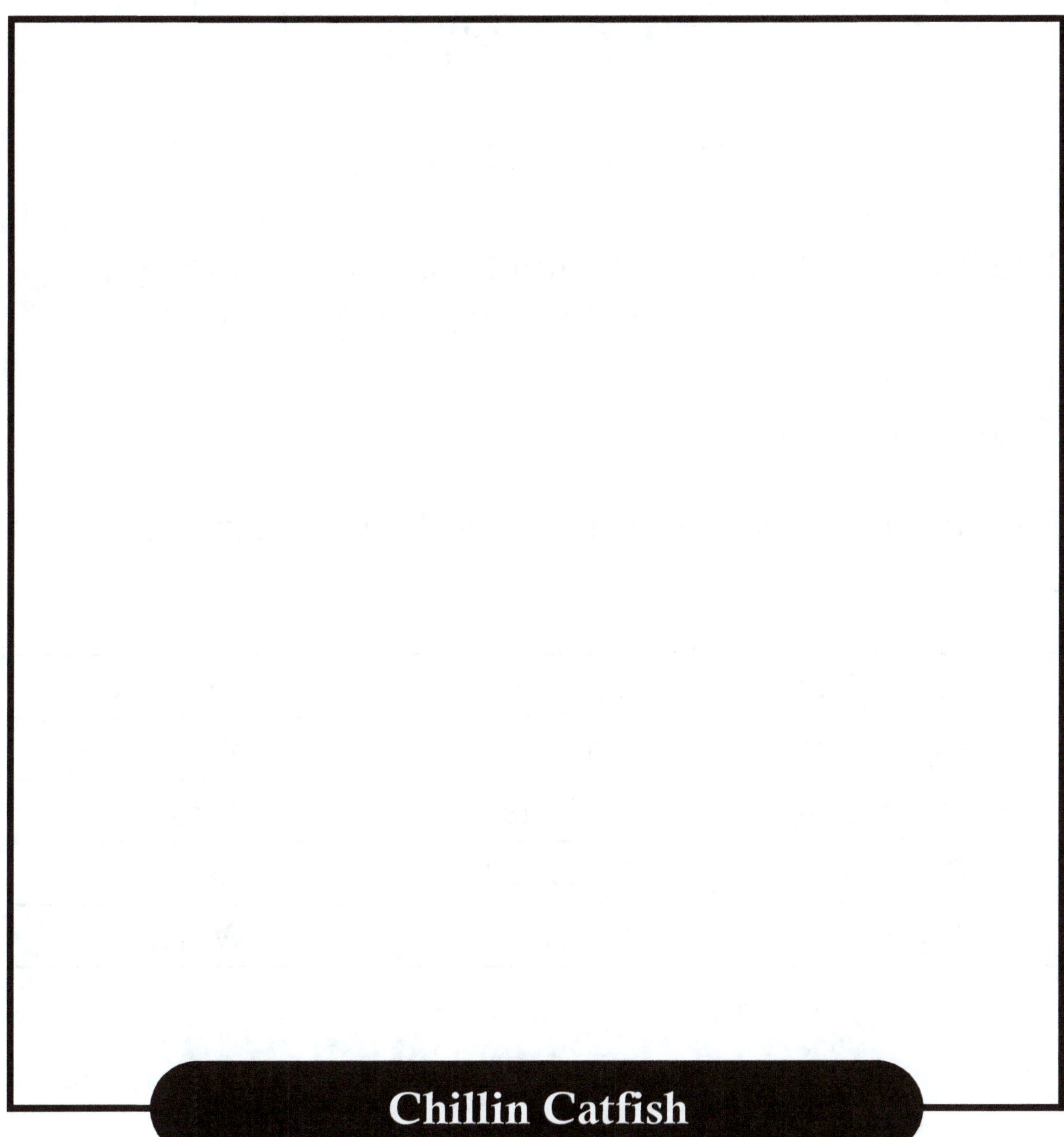

Chillin Catfish

PROMPT 8

Dopey Dachshund

The Task: Draw a dachshund that although long in body, is clearly short on IQ points.

Required Objects:

Incorporate at least three of the following items into your drawing.

Dunce Cap	Knee Pads	Dynamite
Pepper Spray	Taser Gun	Rubber Boots
Electrical Outlet	Toilet	Toaster
Fish Bowl	Hot Dog Bun	Ladder
Fly Paper	Mouse Trap	Whistle

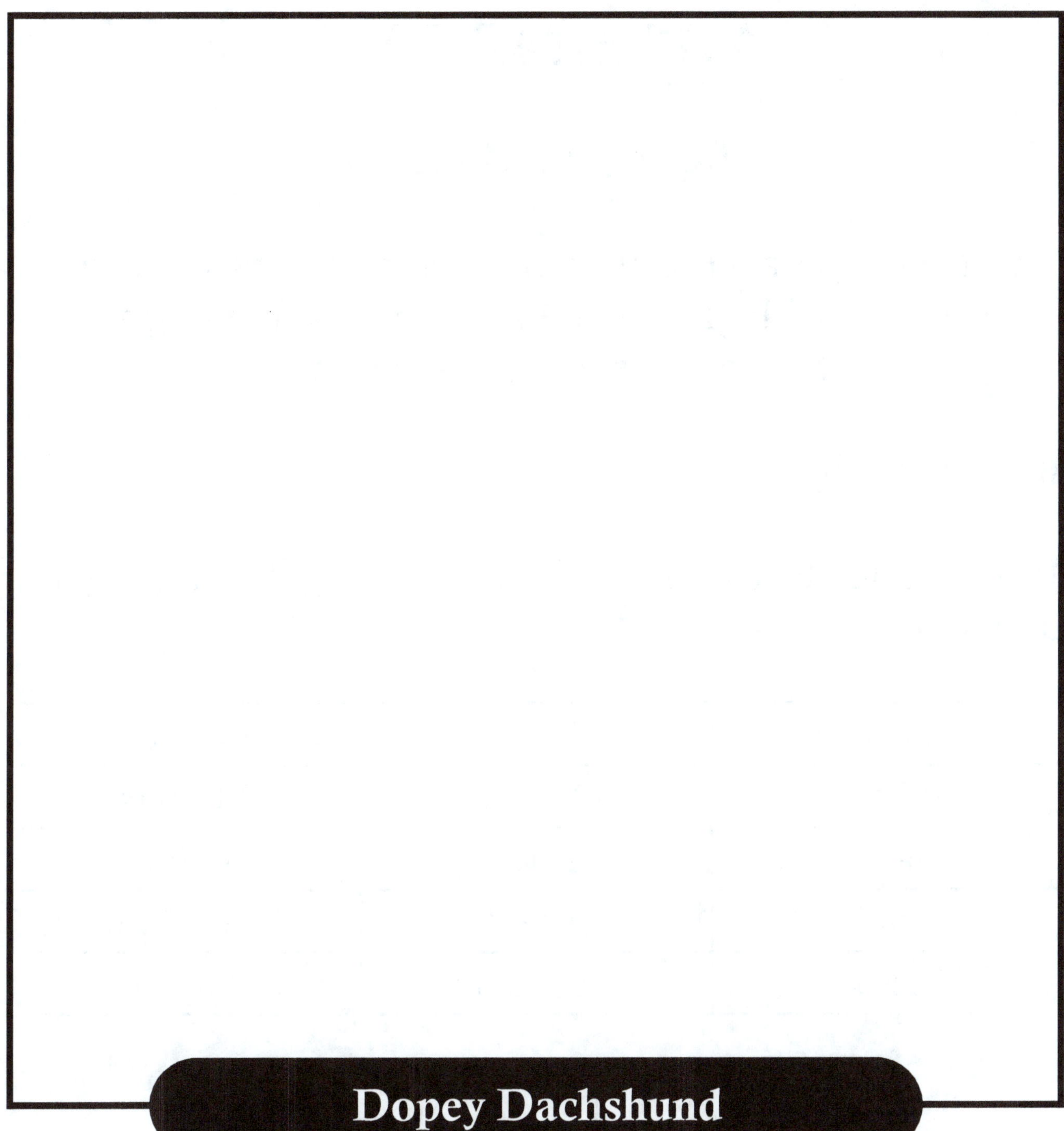

Dopey Dachshund

PROMPT 9

Bereaving Buzzard

The Task:　Draw the kind of buzzard that is so filled with grief it actually buries and eulogizes the dead instead of eating them.

Required Objects:

Incorporate at least three of the following items into your drawing.

Tombstone	Bible	Shovel
Dirt Mound	Holy Water	Flowers
Casket	Pews	Pulpit
Thurible	Tissue Box	Wine Bottle
Cassock	Bag of Lime	Organ

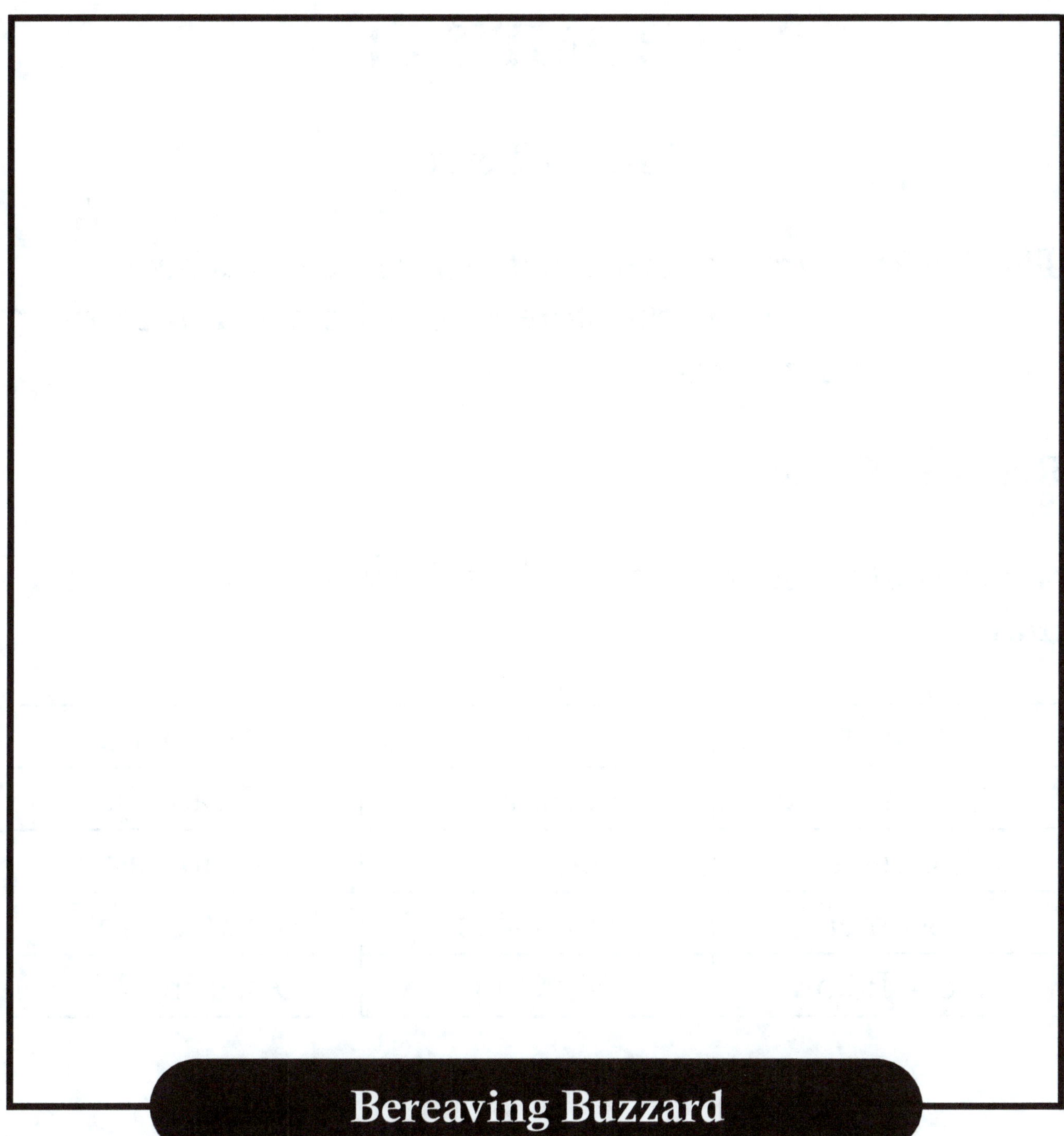

Bereaving Buzzard

PROMPT 10

Flabby Ferret

The Task: Draw a ferret that looks like it has been living in the store room of a donut factory for the past two years.

Required Objects:

Incorporate at least three of the following items into your drawing.

Donuts	Towel	Headband
Weight Scale	Pizza Box	Treadmill
Couch	Television	Chip Bag
Scooter	Hot Dogs	Game Controller
Neck Pillow	Big Gulp	Measuring Tape

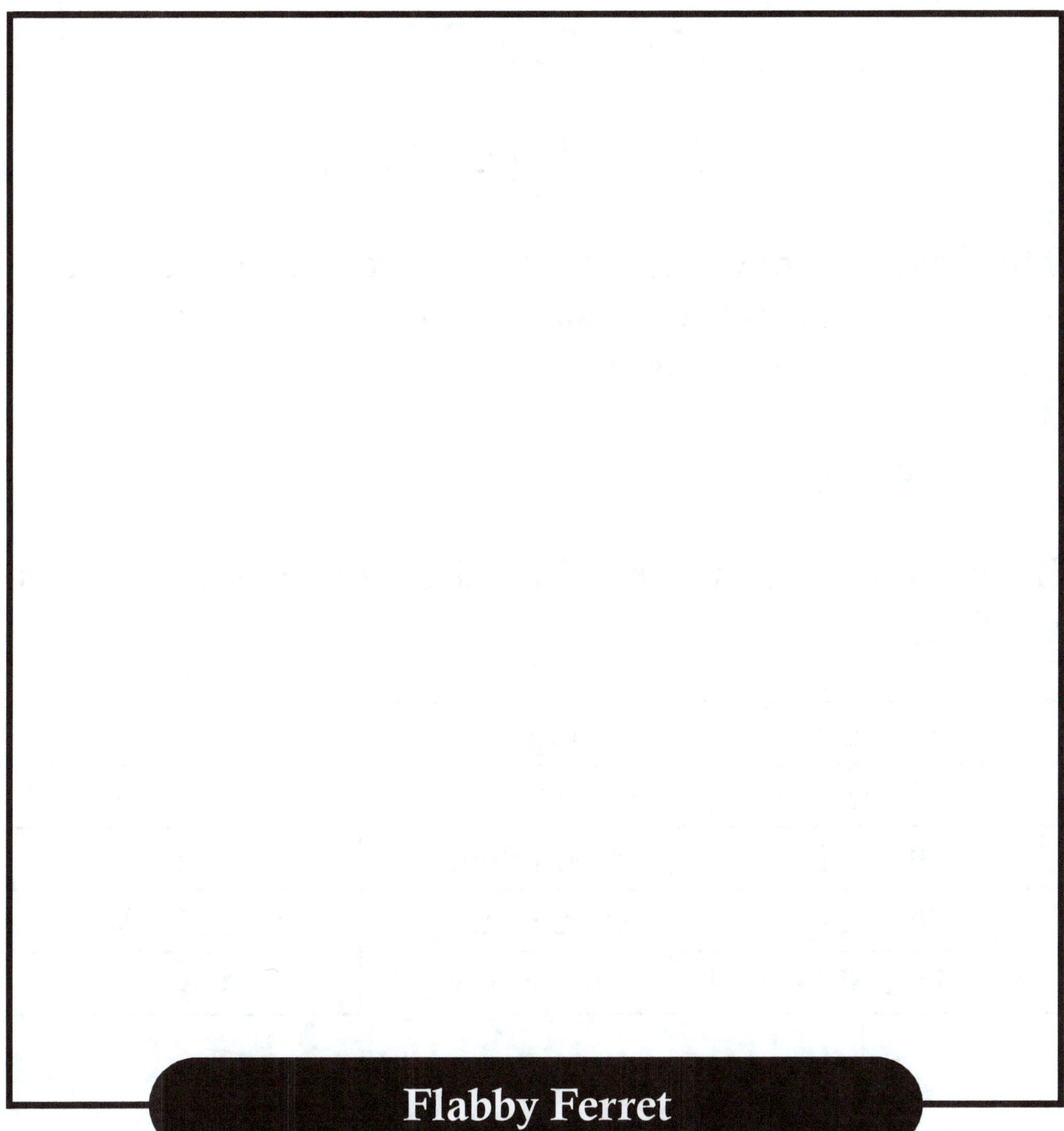

PROMPT 11

Gambling Goose

The Task: Draw a goose that has a pocket full of coin, an ace up its sleeve and is ready to hit the Las Vegas strip.

Required Objects:

Incorporate at least three of the following items into your drawing.

Coin Purse	Playing Cards	Poker Chips
Dice	Slot Machine	Bow Tie
Dollar Bills	Neon Sign	Vest
Cherries	Horse Shoe	Keno Ticket
Roulette Wheel	Sunglasses	Cigar

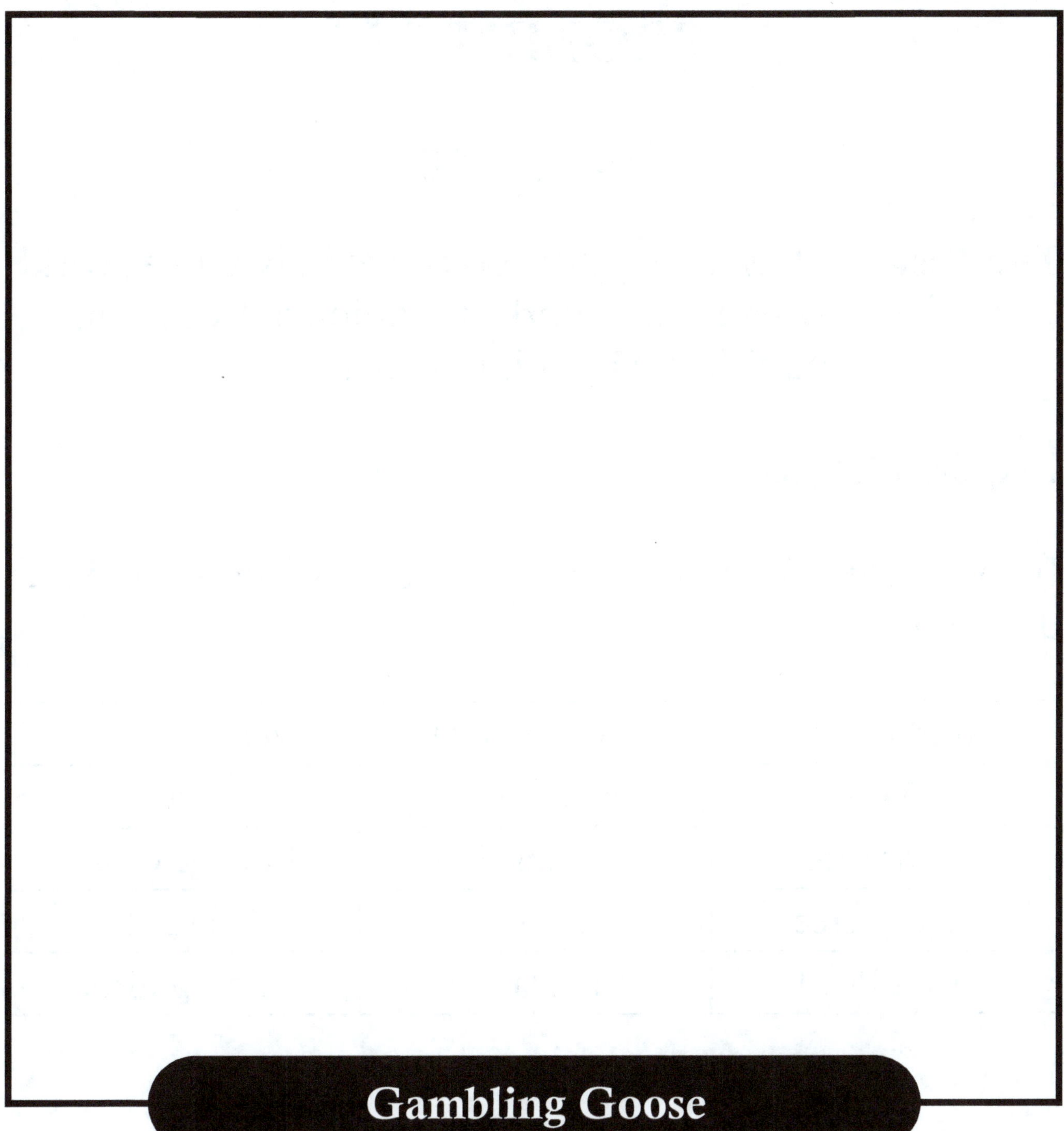

Gambling Goose

PROMPT 12

Happy Hog

The Task: Draw a hog that looks like it lives in a world where eating pork is prohibited by law and punishable by spit roasting.

Required Objects:

Incorporate at least three of the following items into your drawing.

Mud Puddle	Water Trough	Vegan T-shirt
Barn	Wood Fence	Hay
Rotisserie	Warning Sign	Lounge Chair
Shady Tree	Radio	Umbrella
Fruit Bowl	Sunglasses	Camp Fire

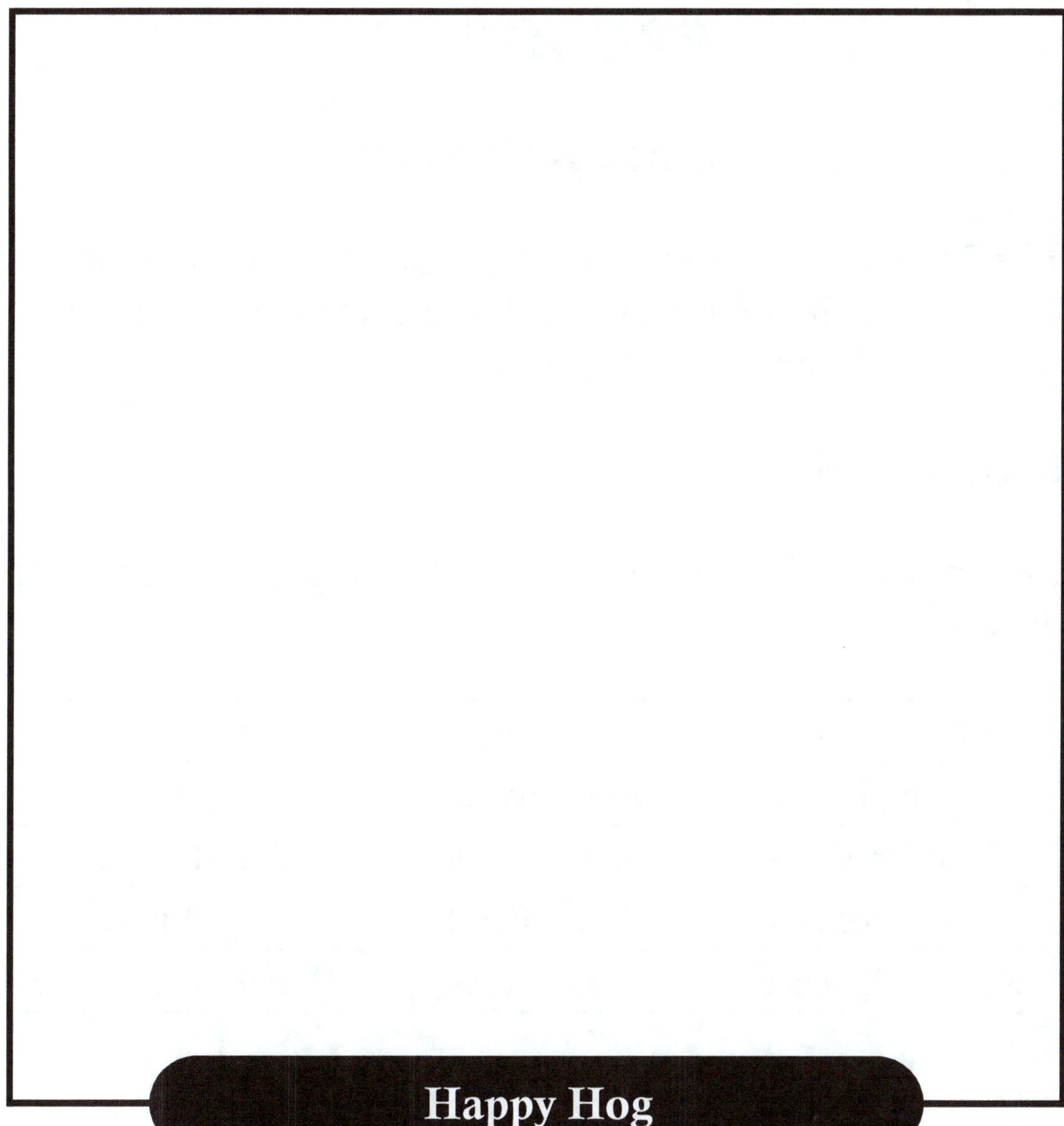

Happy Hog

PROMPT 13

Clueless Chicken

The Task: Draw the kind of chicken that is so out to lunch it actually thinks a rotisserie oven is a sauna for chickens.

Required Objects:

Incorporate at least three of the following items into your drawing.

Rotisserie Oven	Towels	Sandals
Basting Brush	Bag of Feathers	BBQ Sauce
Shower Cap	Cold Drink	Portable Fan
Thermostat	Palm Plant	KFC Bucket
Kitchen Utensils	Spice Rack	Butter On A Rope

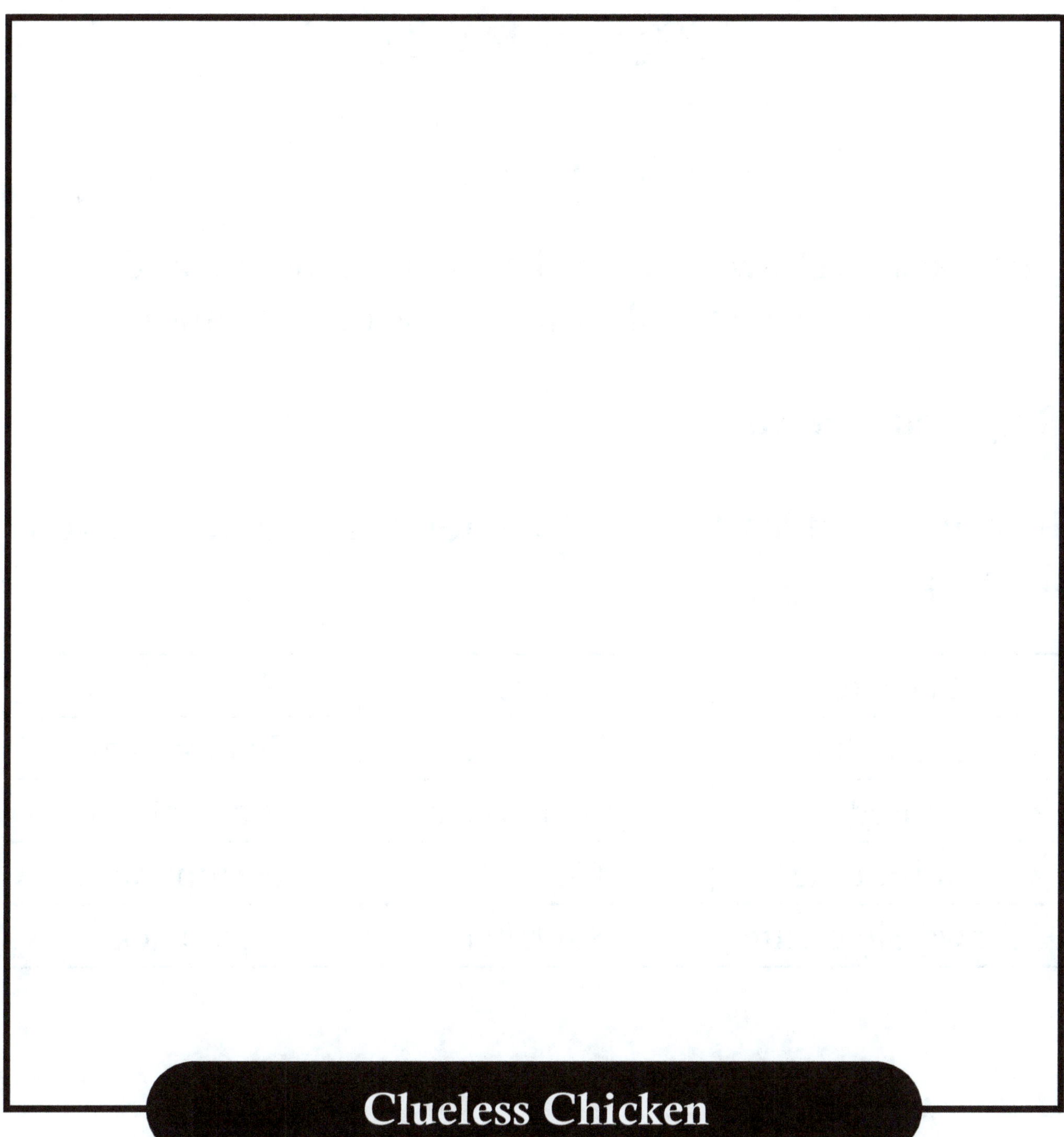

Clueless Chicken

PROMPT 14

Jogging Jaguar

The Task: Draw a jaguar that is all geared up and ready to take on the Boston Marathon.

Required Objects:

Incorporate at least three of the following items into your drawing.

Sneakers	Towel	Sweat Band
Track Suit	Barricade	Fanny Pack
iPod	Sports Watch	Water Bottle
Finish Line	Confetti	Headphones
Crowd Silhouette	Stretcher	Ice Pack

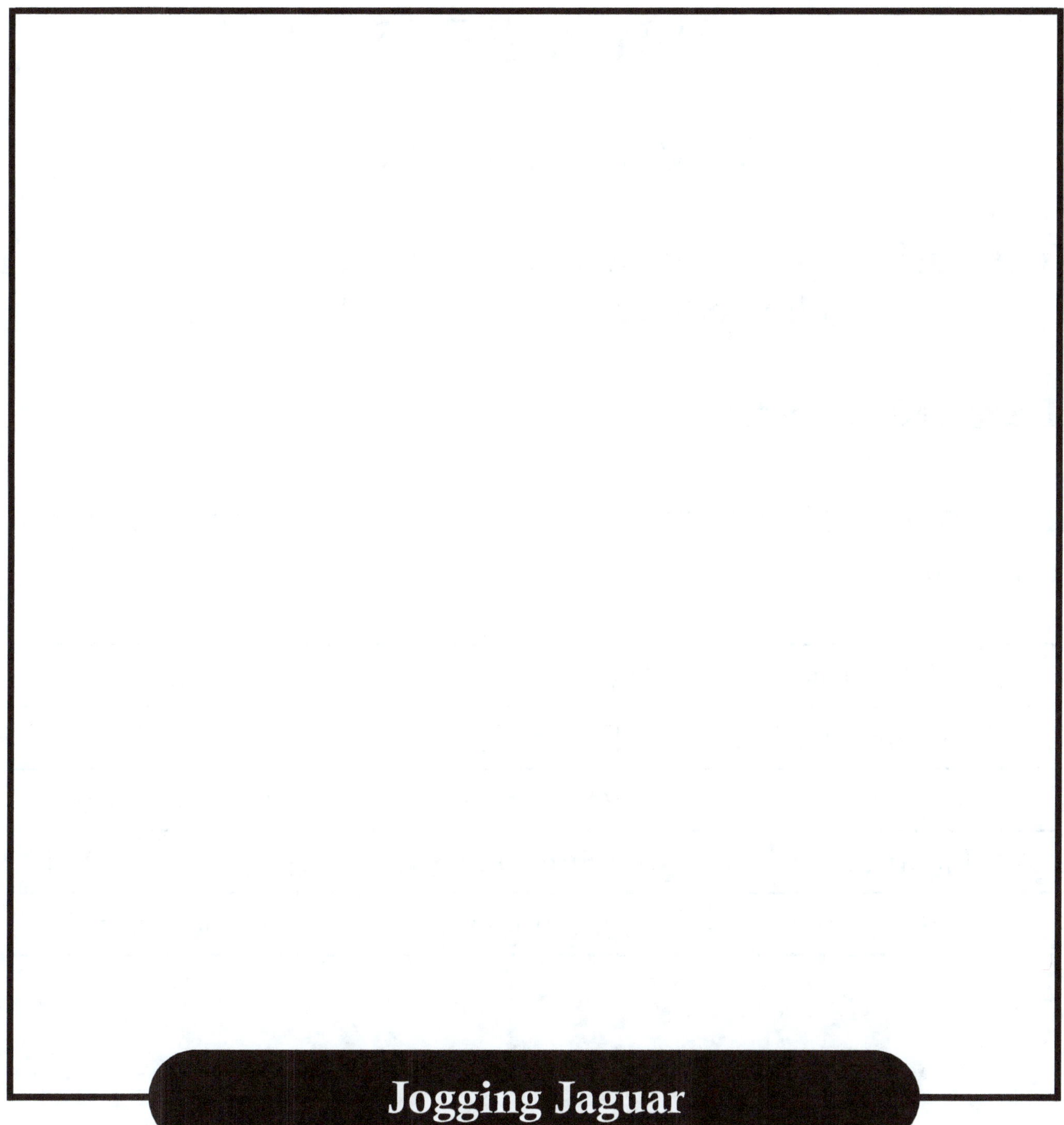

Jogging Jaguar

PROMPT 15

Kickboxing Kangaroo

The Task: Draw a kangaroo that looks like it just climbed into the cage at a UFC event.

Required Objects:

Incorporate at least three of the following items into your drawing.

MMA Gloves	Wooden Stool	Towel
Mouth Guard	Speed Bag	Heavy Bag
Bucket	Water Bottle	Smelling Salts
Head Gear	Sparring Dummy	Ring Corner Pad
Fight Shorts	Sparring Bell	Ankle Brace

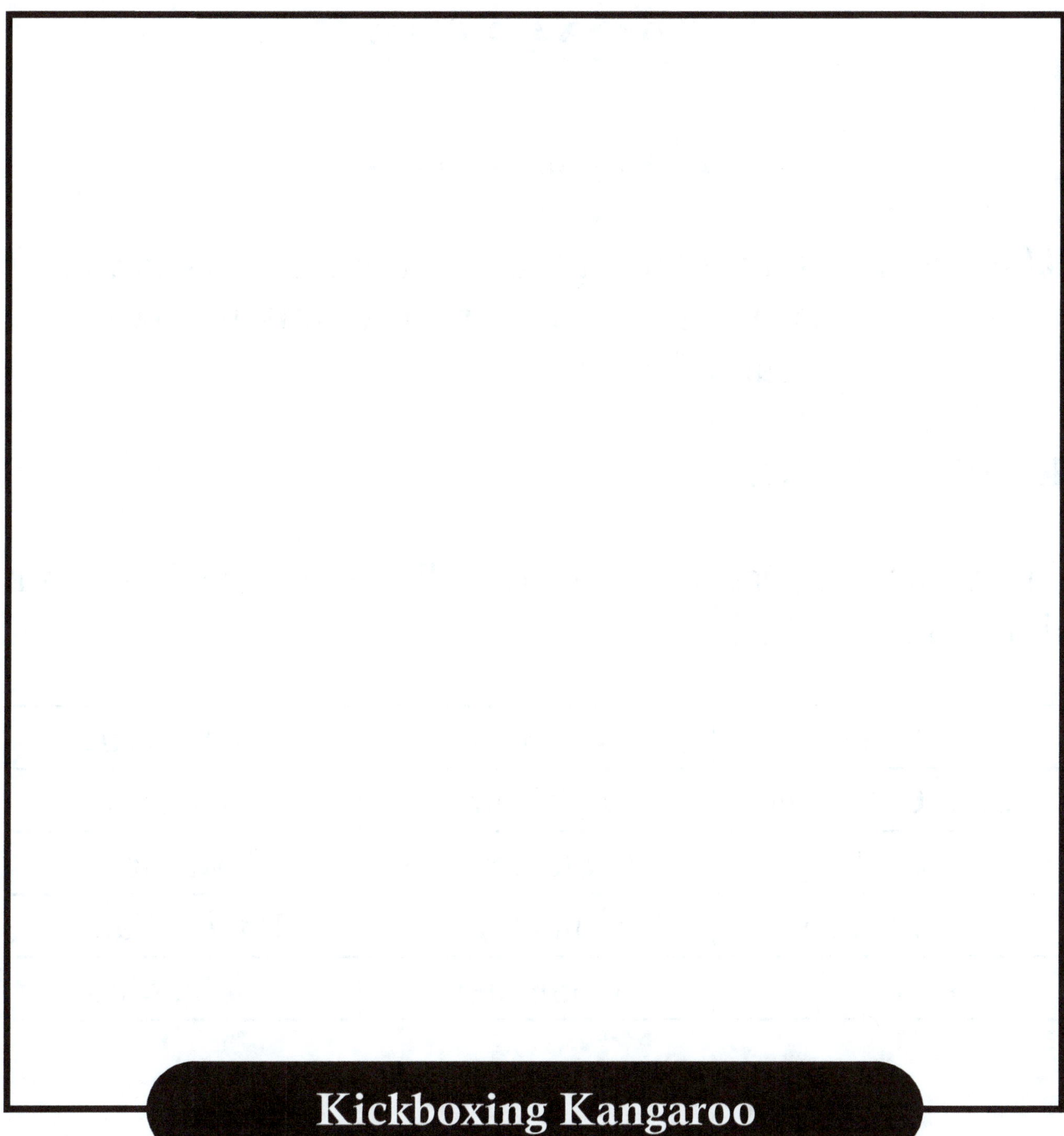

Kickboxing Kangaroo

PROMPT 16

Librarian Locust

The Task: Draw a locust that has book smarts as well as an intolerance for voices talking above a certain decibel level.

Required Objects:

Incorporate at least three of the following items into your drawing.

Books	Eye Glasses	Library Card
Card Catalogue	Desk Lamp	Chair
Desk	Stapler	Newspaper
Book Shelf	Quiet Sign	Potted Plant
Book Cart	Computer	Globe Map

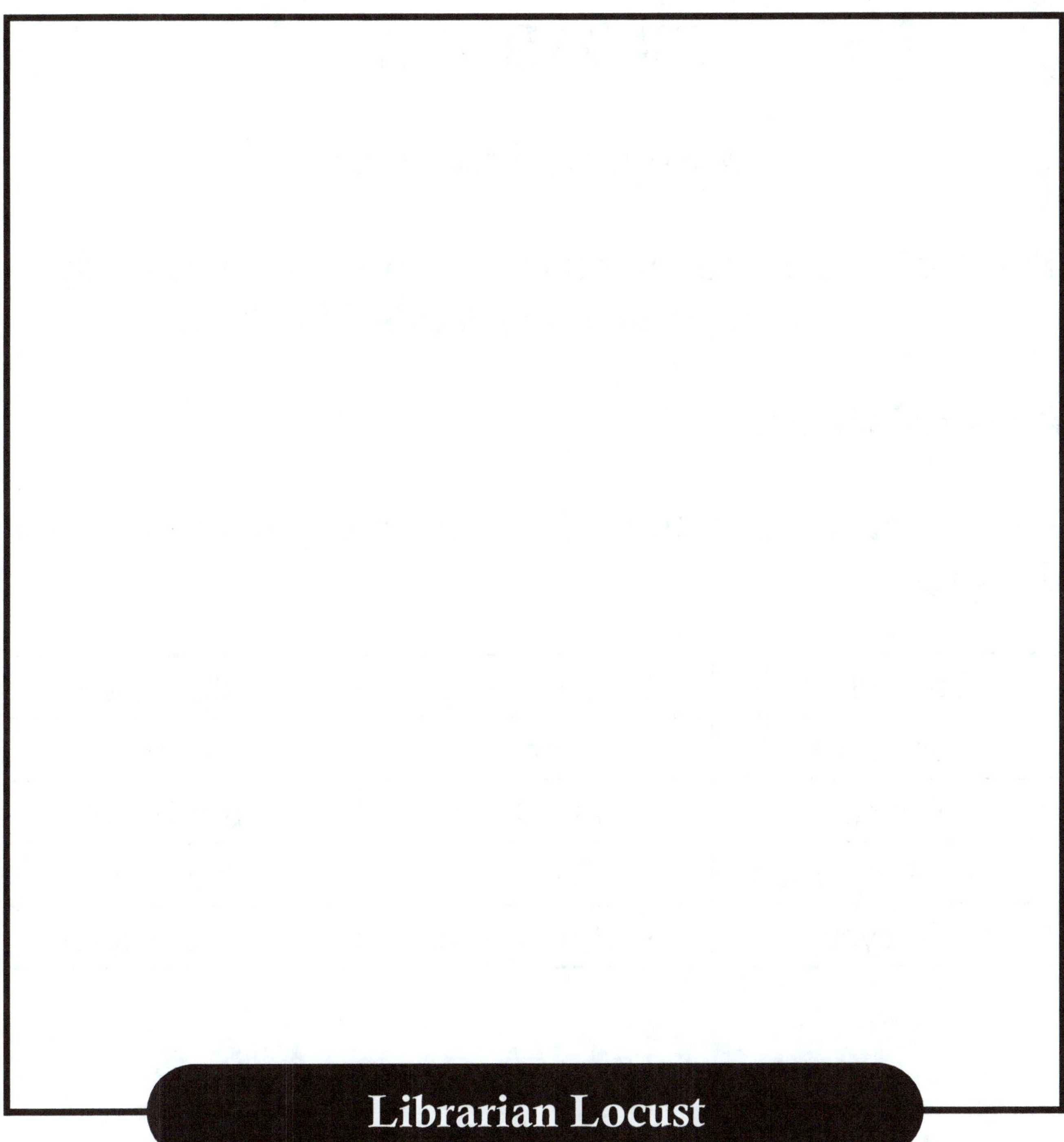

Librarian Locust

PROMPT 17

Marching Minotaur

The Task: Draw a minotaur that looks like it is ready to lead the entire Macy's Day Parade.

Required Objects:

Incorporate at least three of the following items into your drawing.

Busby Hat	Feather Plume	Leader Jacket
Flag Pole	Sabre	Baton
Whistle	Bass Drum	Trombone
Cartoon Balloon	Banner	Popcorn
Unicycle	Cotton Candy	Detour Sign

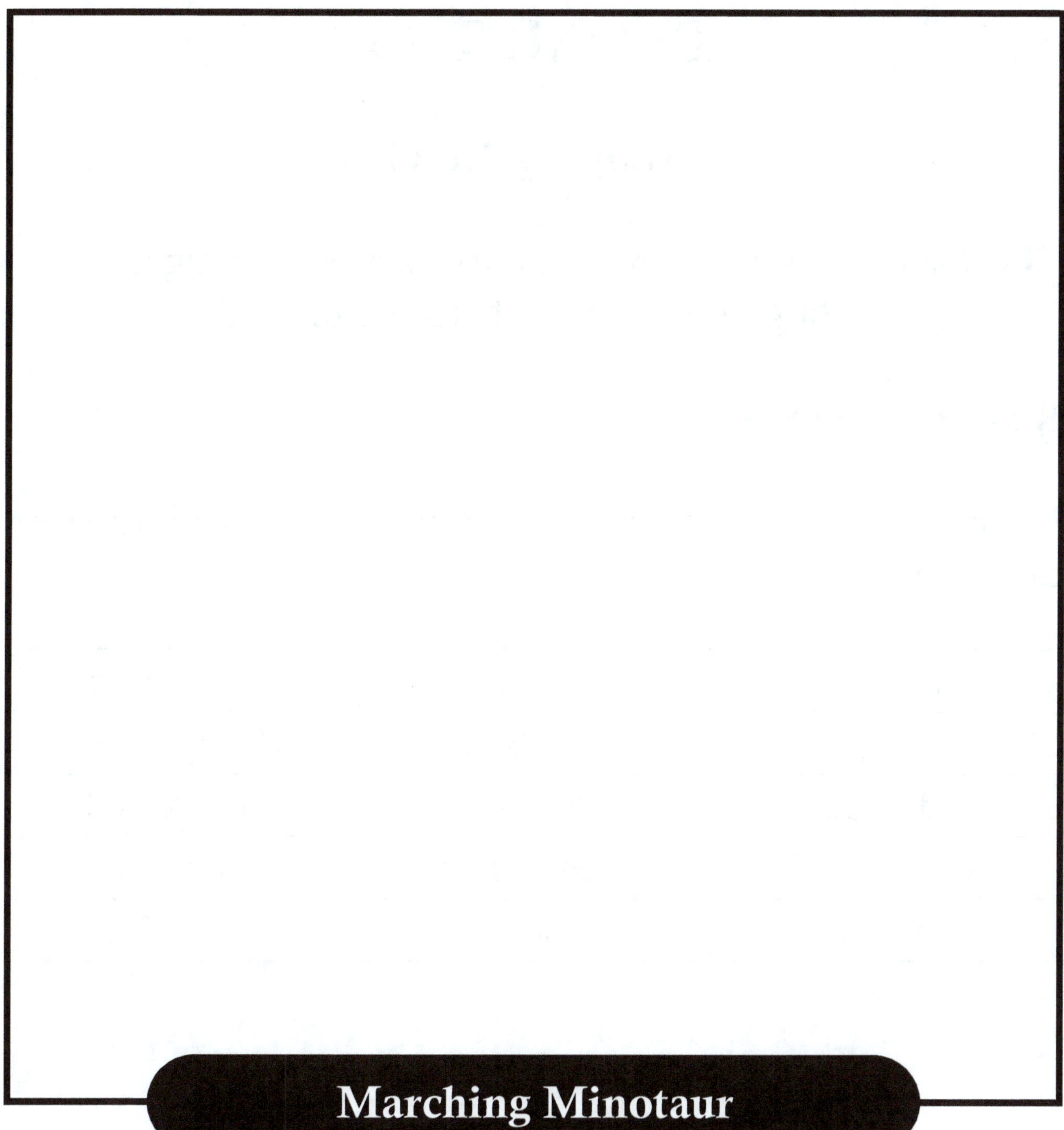

Marching Minotaur

PROMPT 18

Napping Newt

The Task: Draw a newt that appears to be snug as a bug and drifting off to dreamland.

Required Objects:

Incorporate at least three of the following items into your drawing.

Hammock	Pillow	Sleep Mask
Blanket	Story Book	Headphones
Teddy Bear	Pacifier	Music Mobile
Alarm Clock	Night Light	Slippers
Hot Cocoa	Sheep	Night Cap

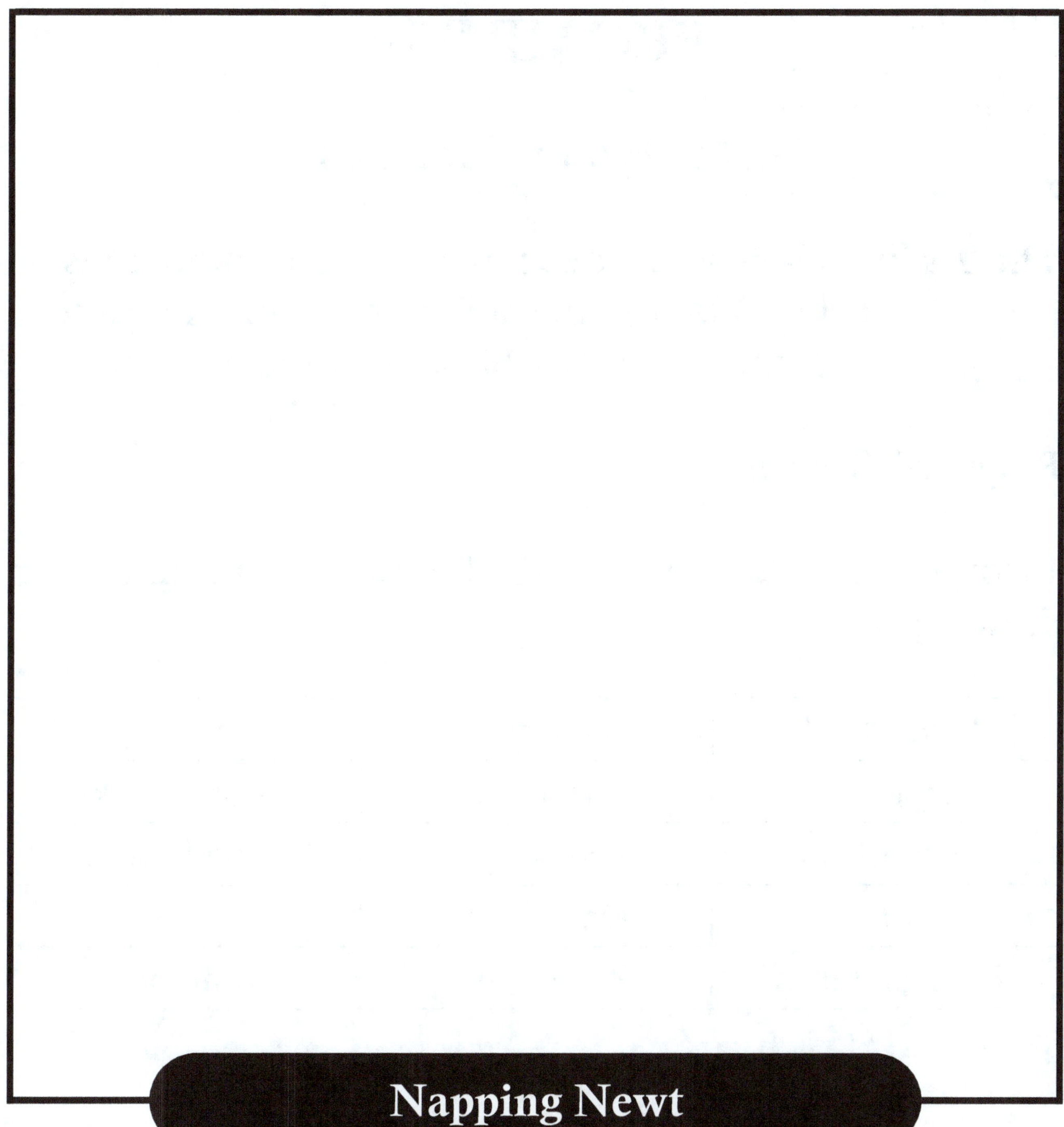

Napping Newt

PROMPT 19

Omnipotent Octopus

The Task: Draw an octopus that due to its numerous tentacles has the ability to do anything and everything all at the same time.

Required Objects:

Incorporate at least three of the following items into your drawing.

Hand Blender	Microphone	Handsaw
Ouija Board	Eye Drops	Story Book
Lawn Mower	Hair Dryer	Boom Box
Camera	Dart Board	Kite
Baseball Glove	Paint Brush	Trampoline

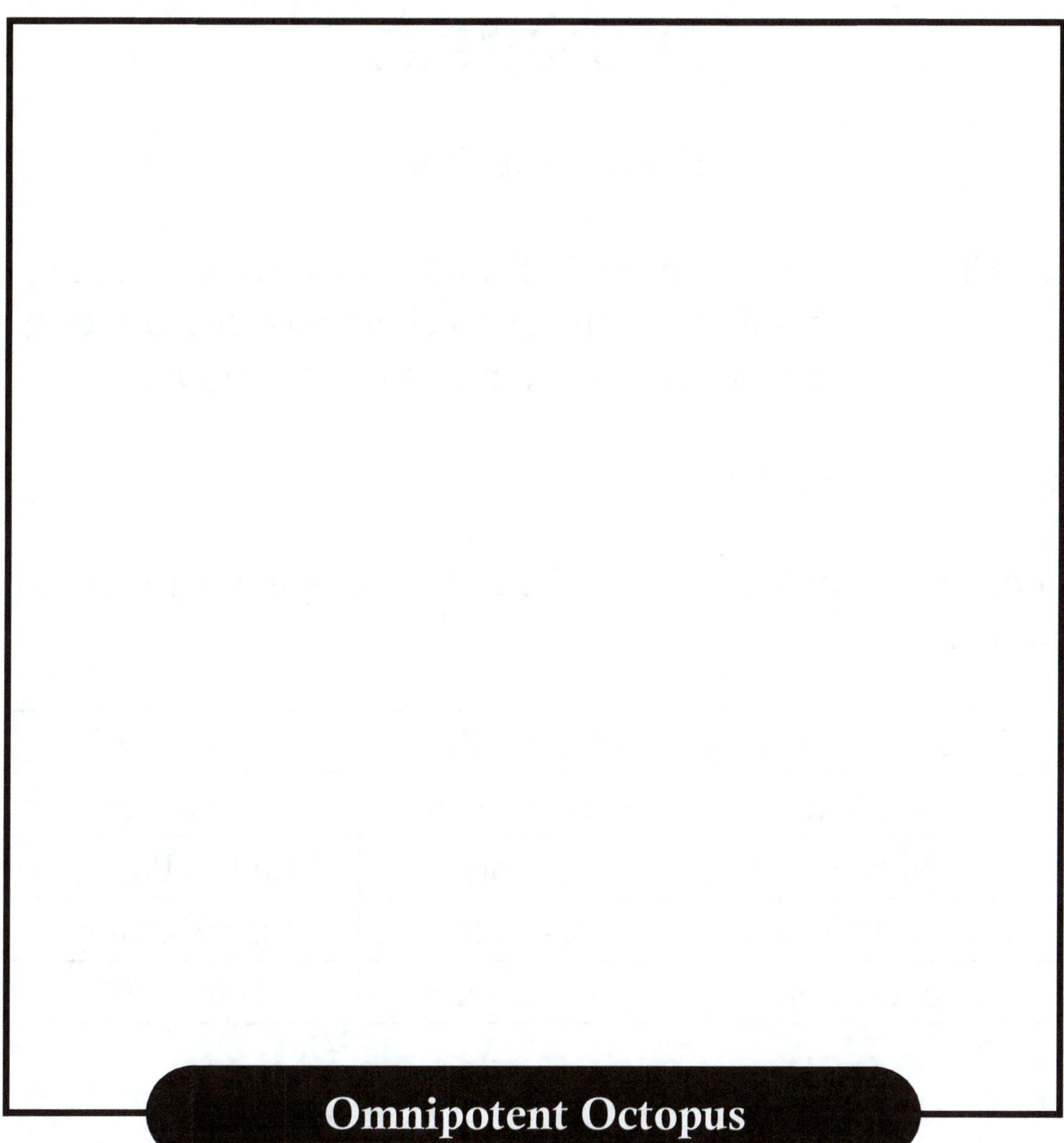
Omnipotent Octopus

PROMPT 20

Dishonest Duck

The Task: Draw the kind of duck that is so deceitful it would actually try to claim wooden hunting decoys as dependents on its tax return.

Required Objects:

Incorporate at least three of the following items into your drawing.

Bounced Check	Donation Box	Credit Cards
Money Bags	Hotel Bathrobe	Used Car
Wallets	Fake Rolex	Ladies Purses
Framed Painting	Passports	Baby's Candy
Election Sign	For Sale Sign	Handcuffs

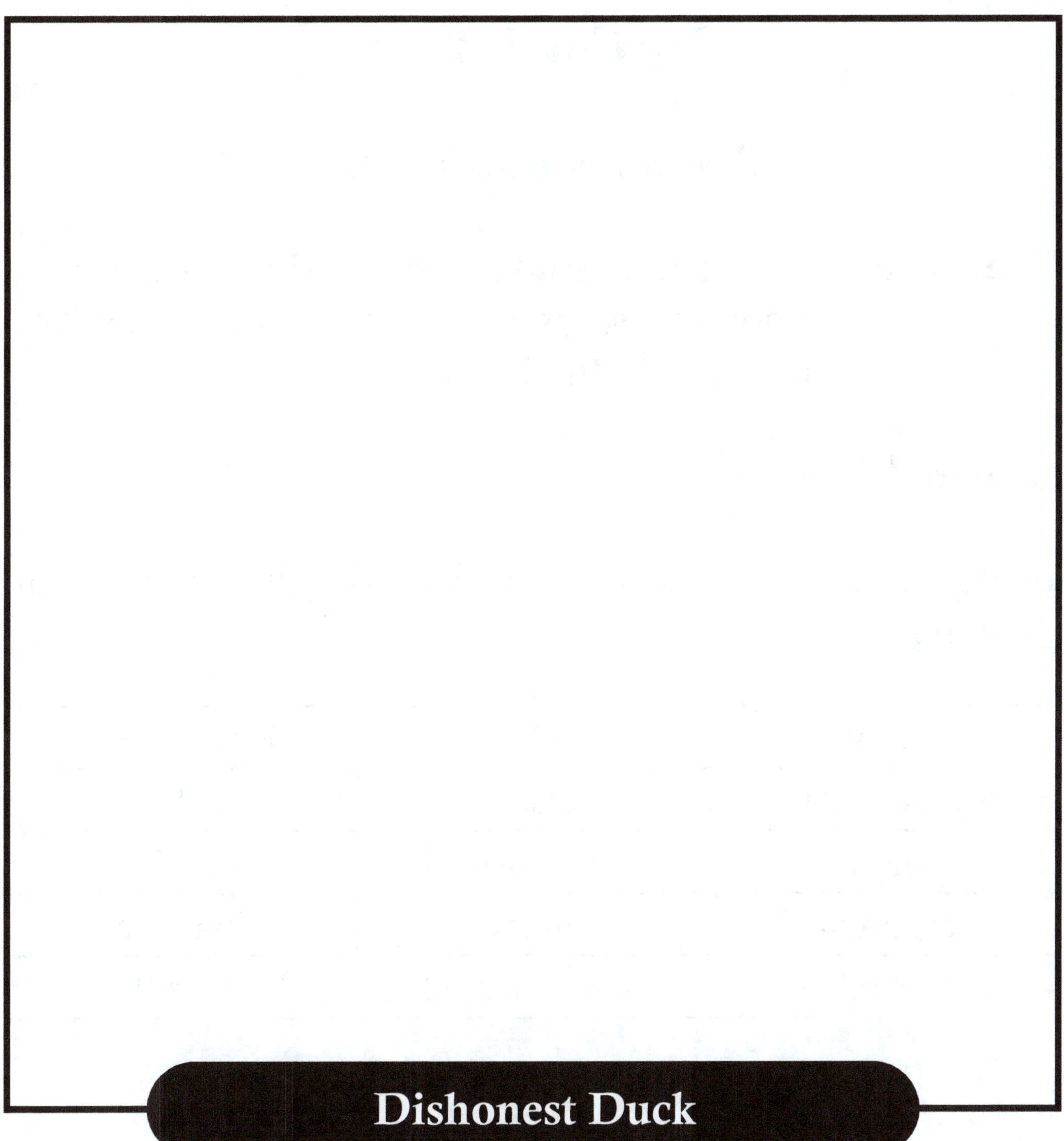

Dishonest Duck

PROMPT 21

Religious Rattlesnake

The Task: Draw a rattlesnake that has shed its unholy venomous ways and now just wants to share the word of the Lord.

Required Objects:

Incorporate at least three of the following items into your drawing.

Cross	Bible	Holy Water
Stained Glass	Rosary	Pulpit
Statue	Chalice	Candle
Menorah	Dreidel	Yamaka
Stone Tablets	Star of David	Scroll

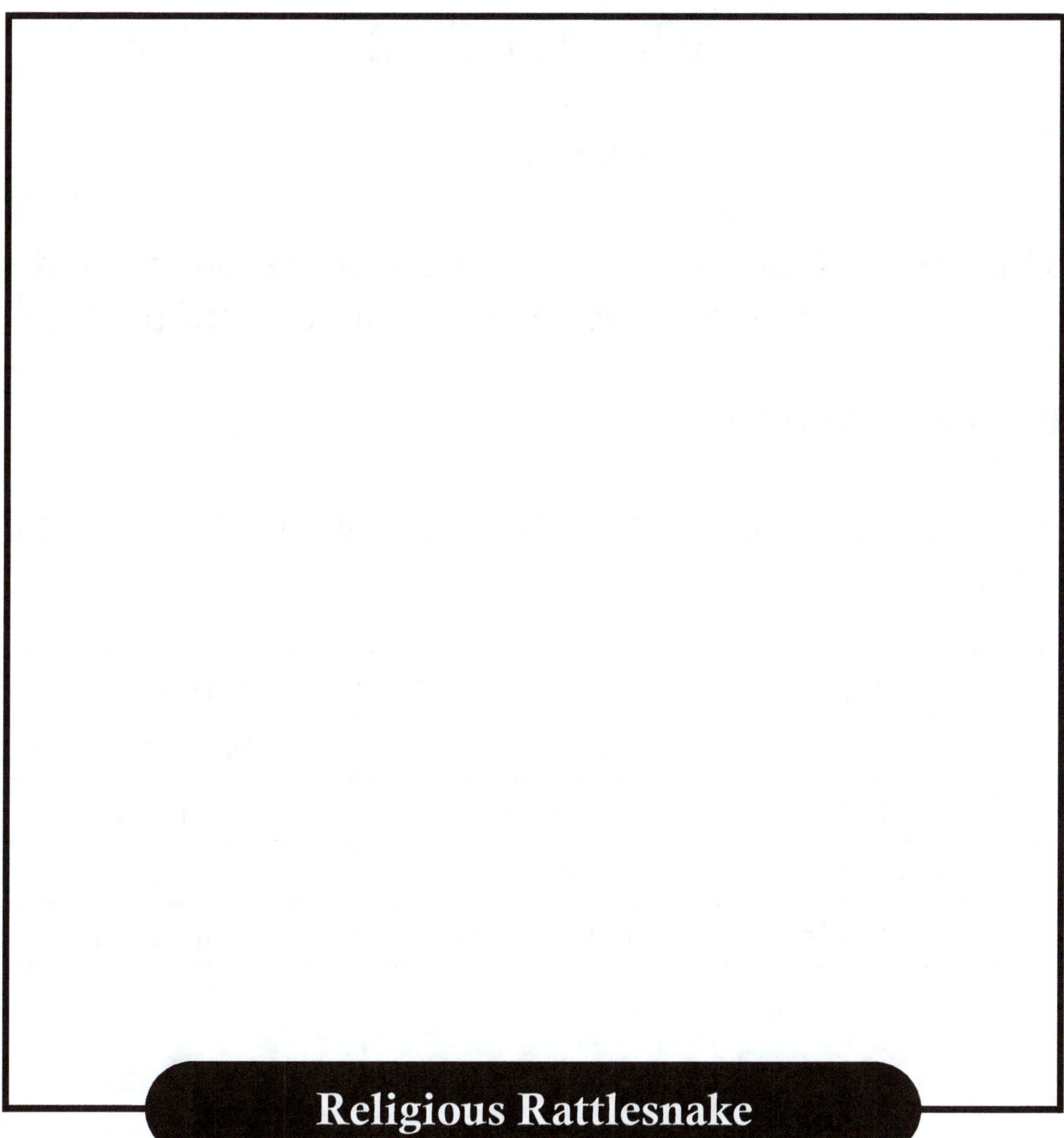

Religious Rattlesnake

PROMPT 22

Crazy Cat

The Task: Draw the type of cat that looks like it could quite possibly be strung out on catnip.

Required Objects:

Incorporate at least three of the following items into your drawing.

Catnip	Rubber Mouse	Yarn Ball
Scratching Post	Liter Box	Elizabethan Collar
Straight Jacket	Muzzle	Laser Pointer
Fish Bowl	Cigarette	Pet Carrier
Handcuffs	Hair Rollers	Chandelier

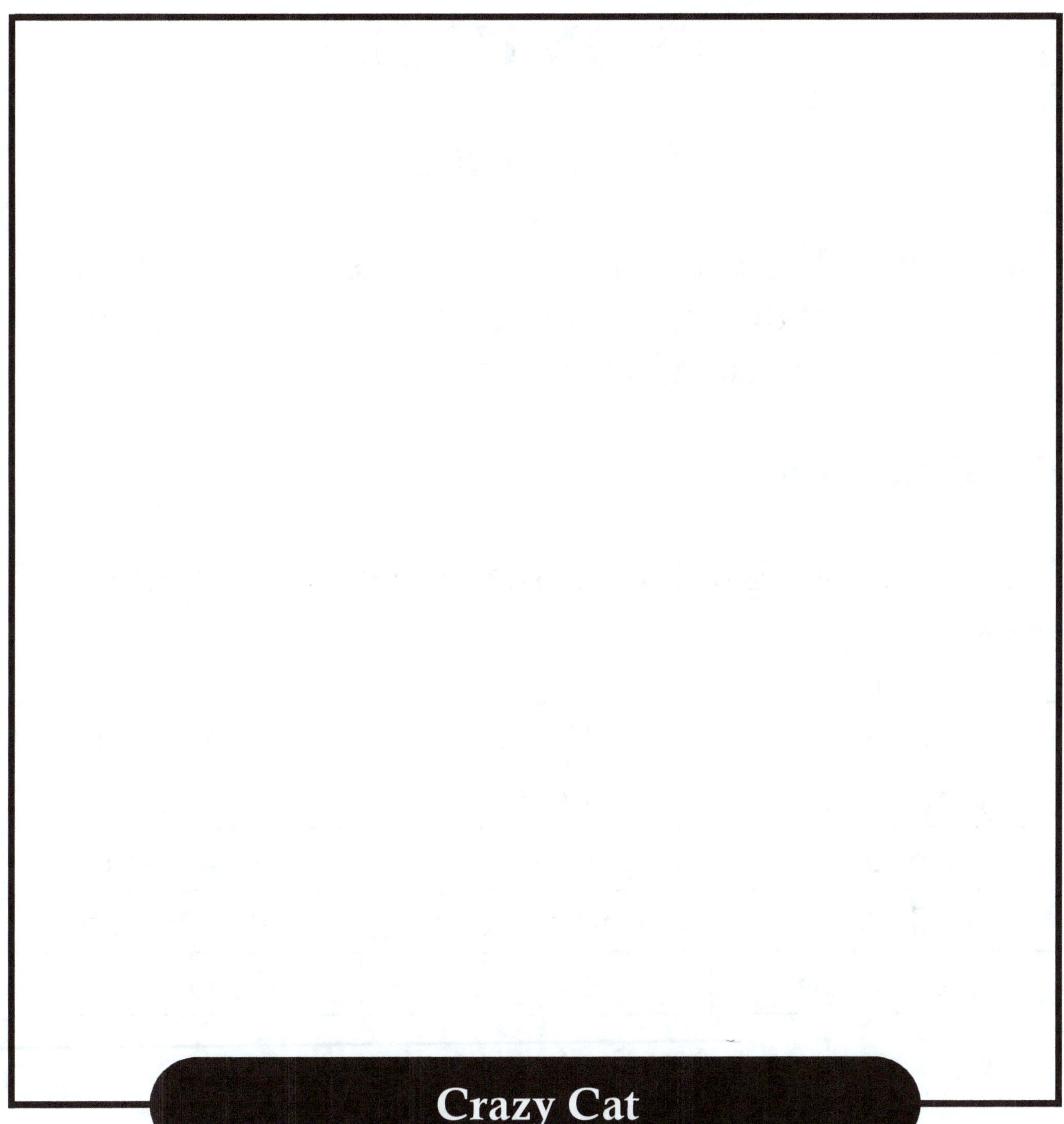

Crazy Cat

PROMPT 23

Salesman Slug

The Task: Draw a slug that looks like it spends its days slithering door to door selling overpriced magazine subscriptions.

Required Objects:

Incorporate at least three of the following items into your drawing.

Briefcase	Fedora	Clip Board
Fountain Pen	White Board	Tie
Contract	Door Bell	Sunglasses
Cell Phone	Encyclopedia	Snake Oil Bottle
Trench Coat	Mustache	Dollar Bills

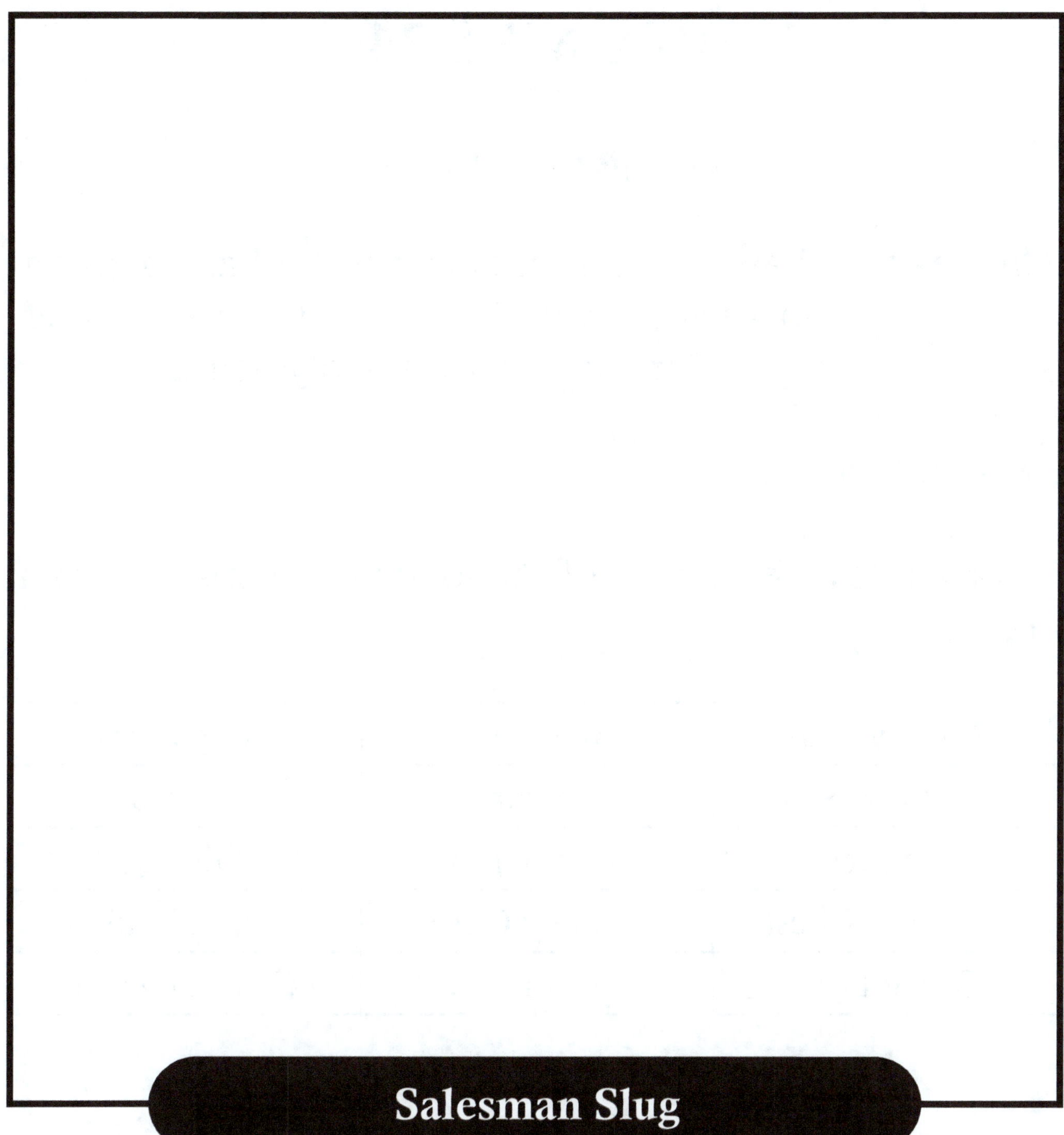

Salesman Slug

PROMPT 24

Prosperous Parrot

The Task: Draw a parrot that looks like it has hotels on Boardwalk, Park Place as well as every other plot of land on the Monopoly board.

Required Objects:

Incorporate at least three of the following items into your drawing.

Money Clip	Gold Chain	Sunglasses
Business Suit	Cigar	Top Hat
Monocle	Money Bag	Oil Rig
Treasure Chest	Fancy Car	Bank Vault
Office Desk	Cane	Cash Register

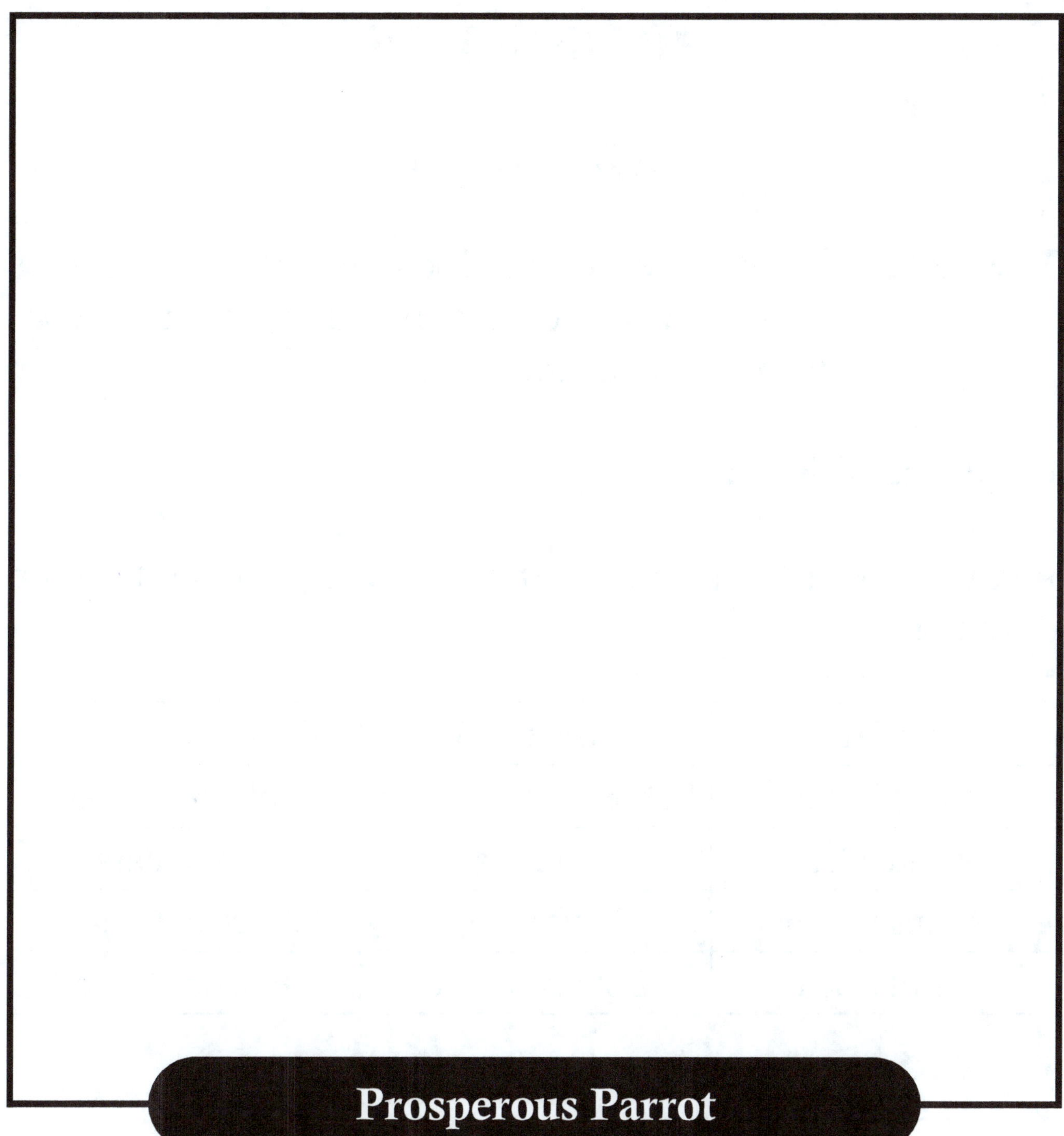

Prosperous Parrot

PROMPT 25

Wily Weasel

The Task: Draw a weasel that looks like it is about to execute a very dastardly plan that will allow it to take over the world.

Required Objects:

Incorporate at least three of the following items into your drawing.

Blue Prints	Detonator Box	Dynamite Sticks
ACME Box	Laboratory Beakers	Rubber Gloves
White Coat	Camera	Binoculars
Mouse Trap	Duffel Bag	Protective Goggles
Utility Belt	Tobacco Pipe	Poison Bottle

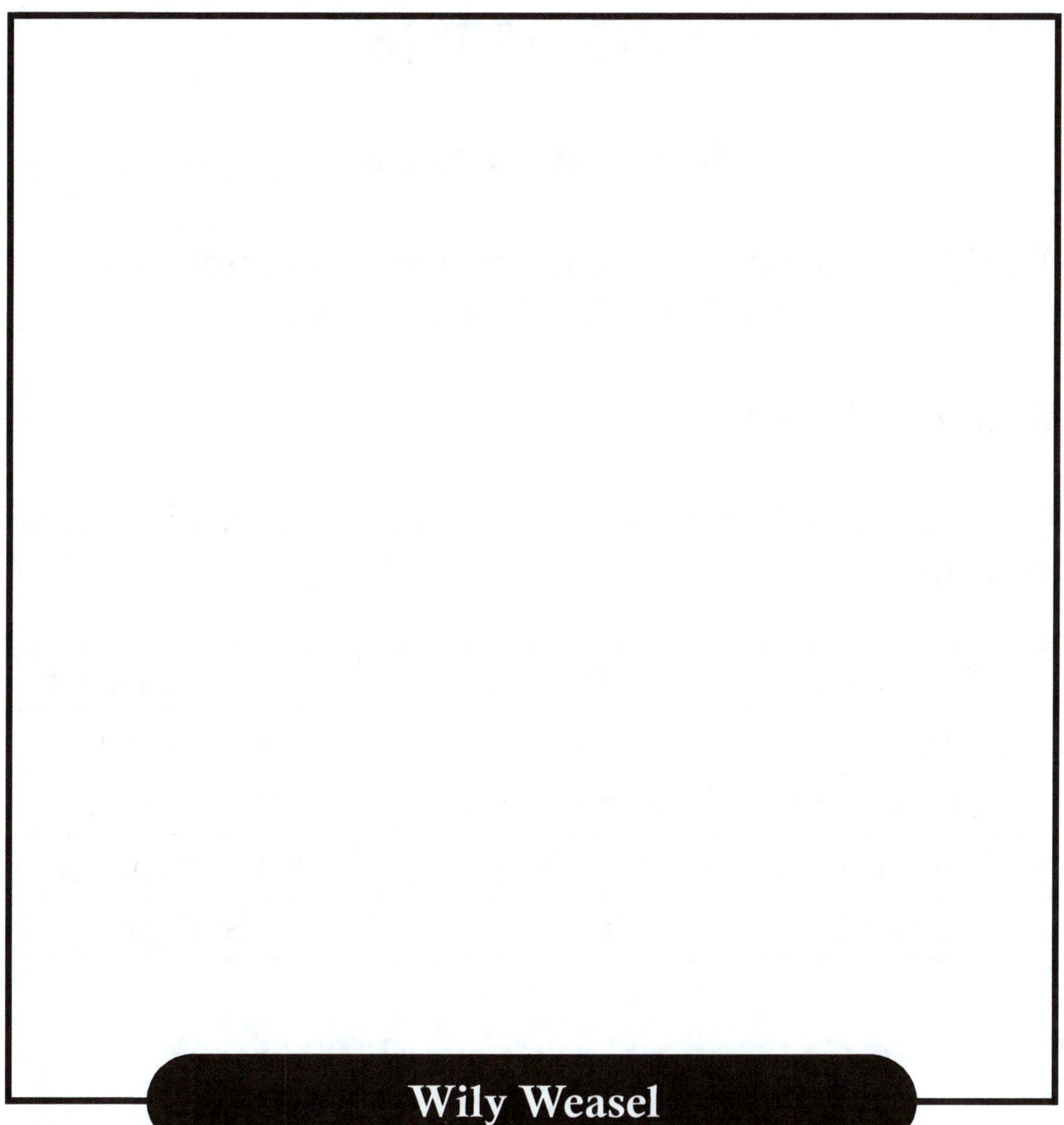

Wily Weasel

PROMPT 26

Terrified Tarantula

The Task: Draw a tarantula that is so cowardly it's actually afraid of its own shadow.

Required Objects:

Incorporate at least three of the following items into your drawing.

Spider Web	Flashlight	Security Blanket
Stuffed Animal	Phobia Book	Storm Cloud
Dentist Drill	Jack-In-The-Box	Water Puddle
Surgical Mask	Coughing Fly	Popping Balloon
Umbrella	Step Ladder	Syringe

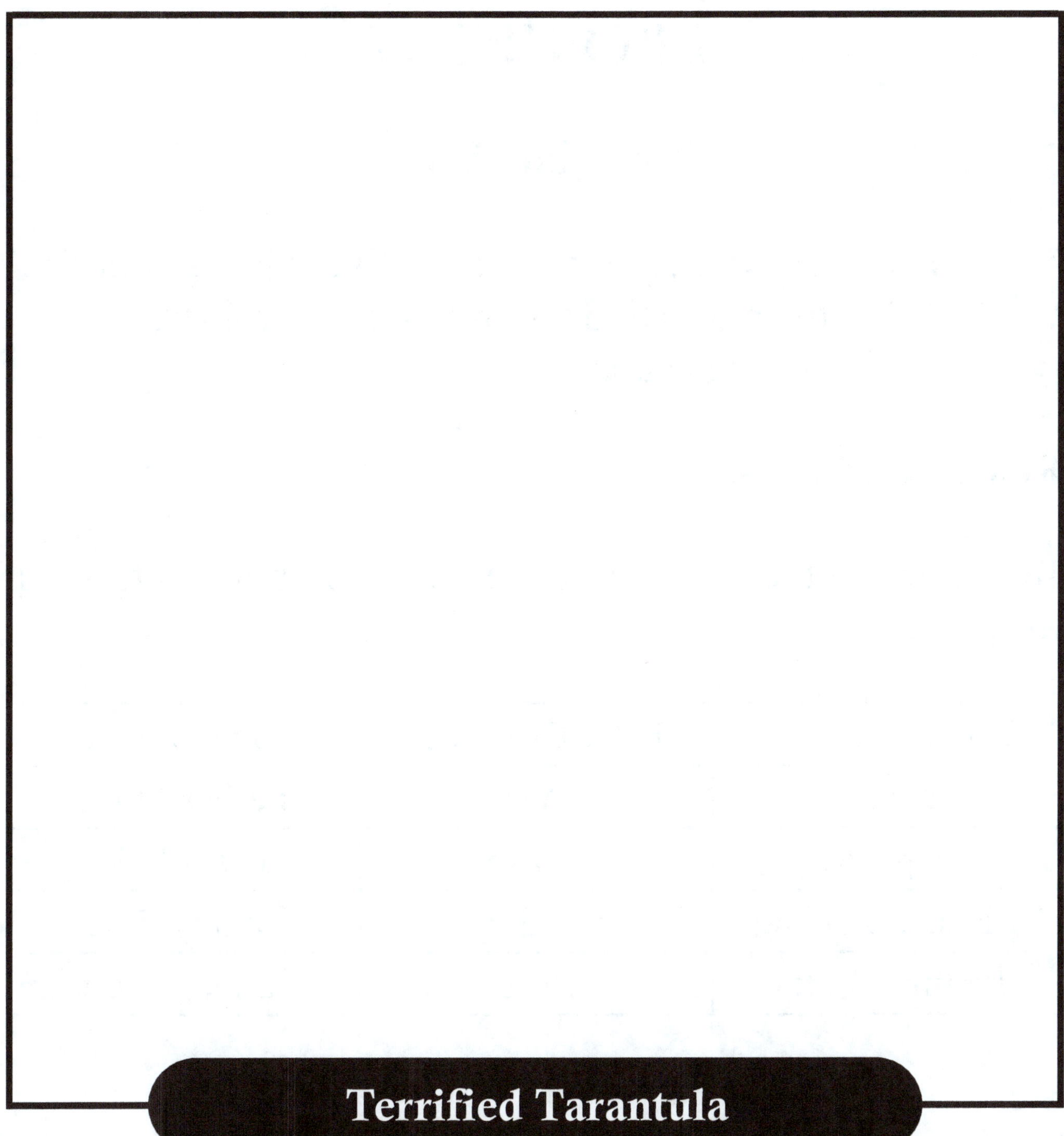

Terrified Tarantula

PROMPT 27

Vivacious Viper

The Task: Draw a viper that looks like it just got back from Marti Gras and had no problem getting beads.

Required Objects:

Incorporate at least three of the following items into your drawing.

Beaded Necklace	False Eyelashes	Hooped Earrings
Bustier	Wig	Ladies Purse
Lipstick	Parasol	Brass Pole
Fishnet Stalking	Lollipop	Bunny Ears
Perfume Bottle	Rose	Champagne Glass

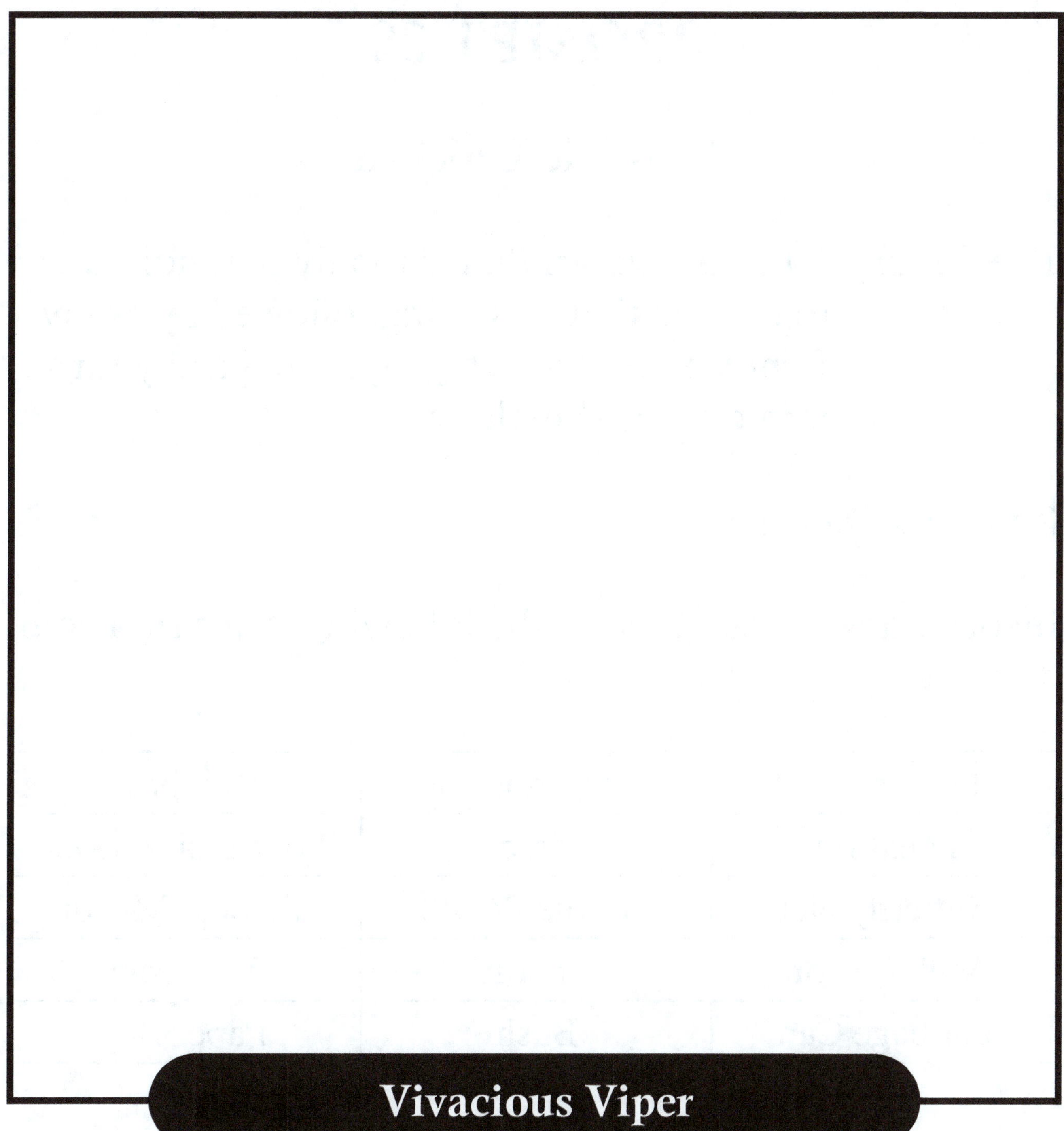

Vivacious Viper

PROMPT 28

Unstable Unicorn

The Task: Draw a unicorn that is totally paranoid due to the fact that it is being followed by a tiny Leprechaun that is trying to magically turn it into a marshmallow.

Required Objects:

Incorporate at least three of the following items into your drawing.

Leprechaun	Cast Iron Pot	Rainbow
Cereal Box	Tree	Four Leaf Clover
Butterfly Net	Large Bowl	Tactical Mirror
Milk Carton	Spoon	Hacksaw
Garbage Can	Bush	Paper Bag

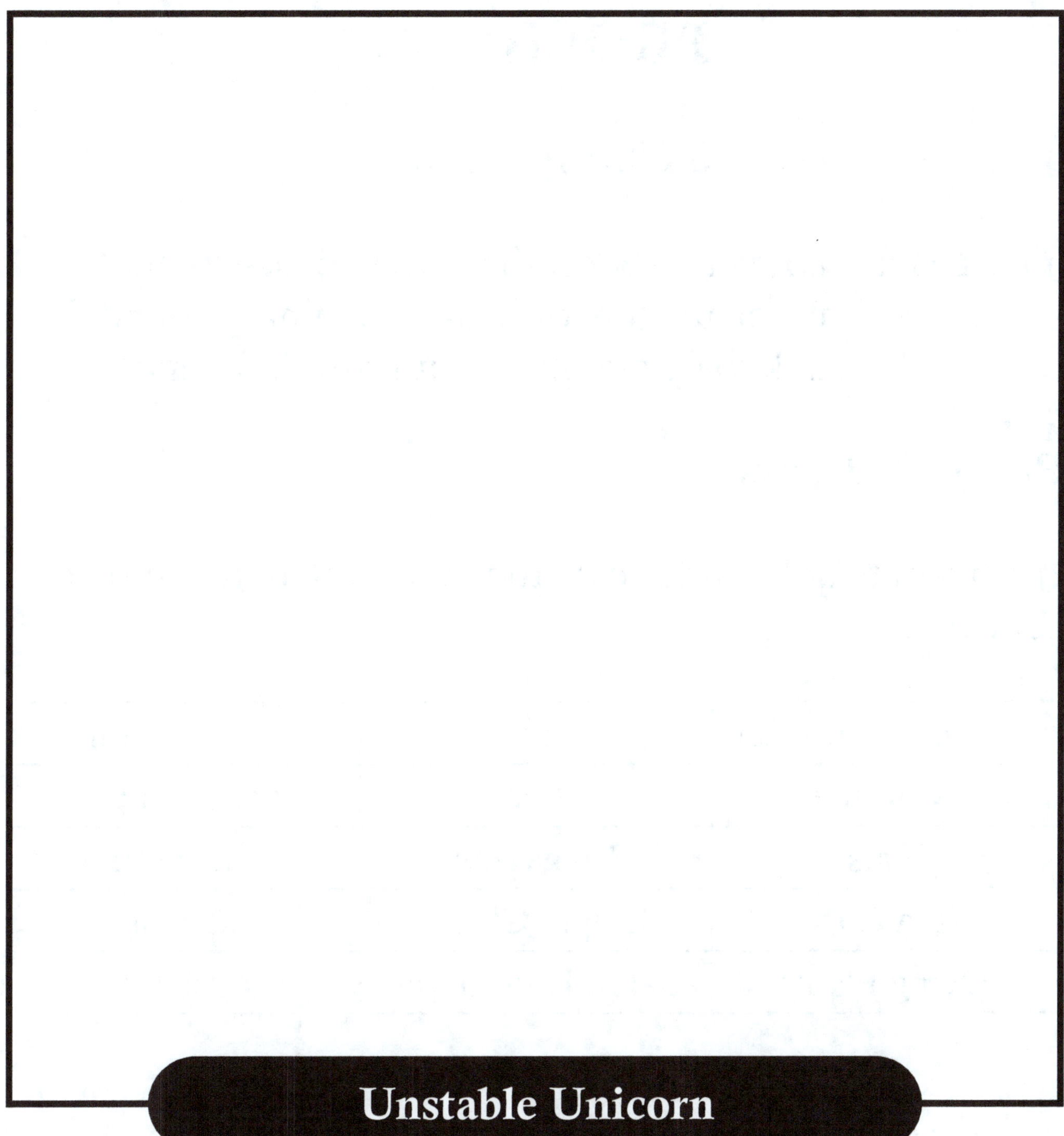

Unstable Unicorn

PROMPT 29

Babbling Baboon

The Task: Draw a baboon that loves to gossip but unfortunately only has imaginary friends to talk to (get creative with the elements).

Required Objects:

Incorporate at least three of the following items into your drawing.

Bluetooth Headset	Salon Chair	Mannequin
Nail File	Balloons	Fuzzy Slippers
Hats	Magazine	Skeleton
Tea Cup	Empty Chairs	Mirror
Dying Plants	Salon Hair Dryer	House Coat

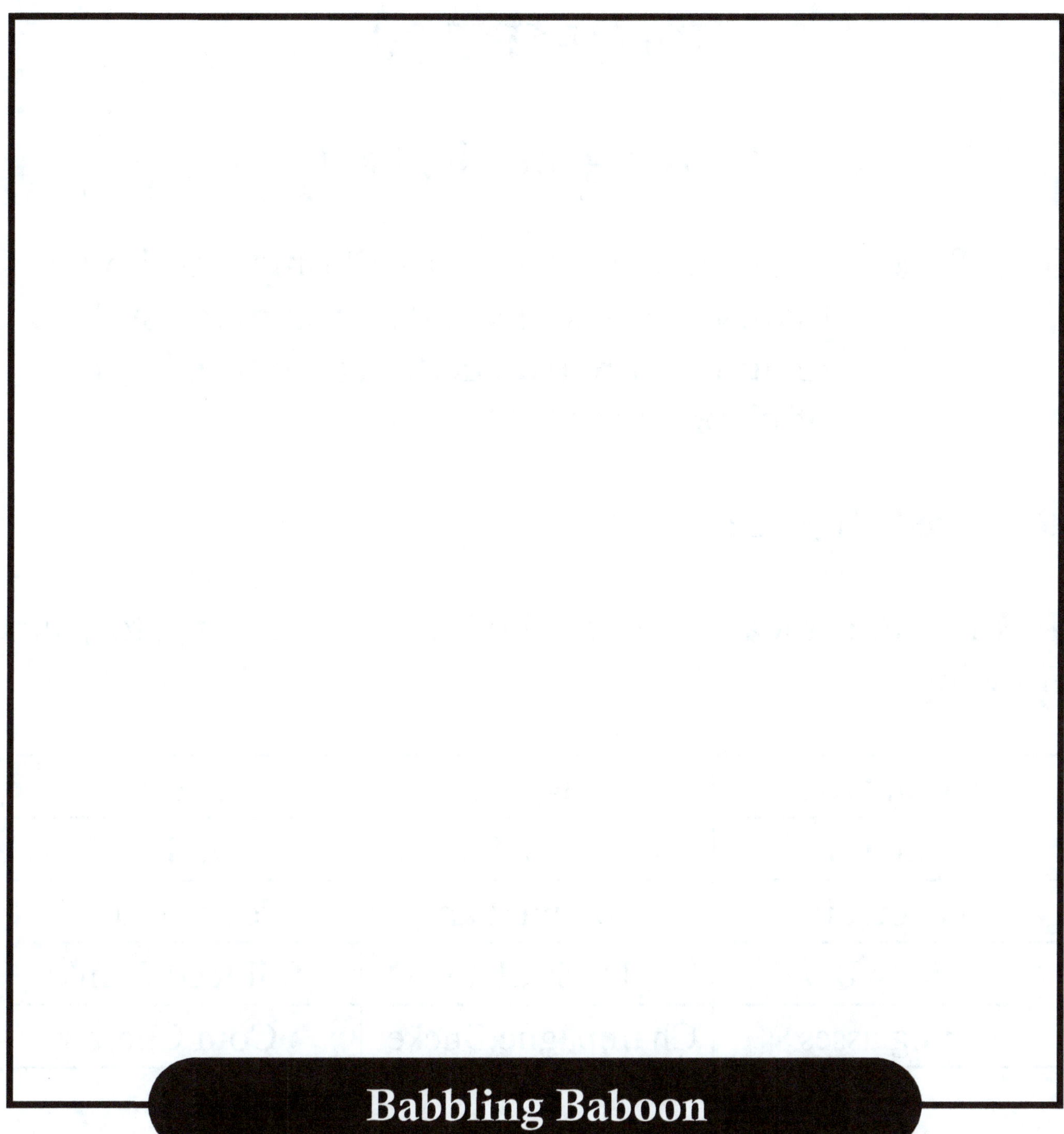

Babbling Baboon

PROMPT 30

Extravagant Elephant

The Task: Draw an elephant that will only travel on luxury cruise ships and has so much stuff it requires more trunks than an entire herd of elephants.

Required Objects:

Incorporate at least three of the following items into your drawing.

Boarding Ramp	Luggage	Jewelry
Parasol	Walking Stick	Sun Hat
Palanquin	Folding Fan	Porter Mice
Candy Box	Deck Chair	Tall Iced Drink
Sunglasses	Champagne Bucket	Coin Chest

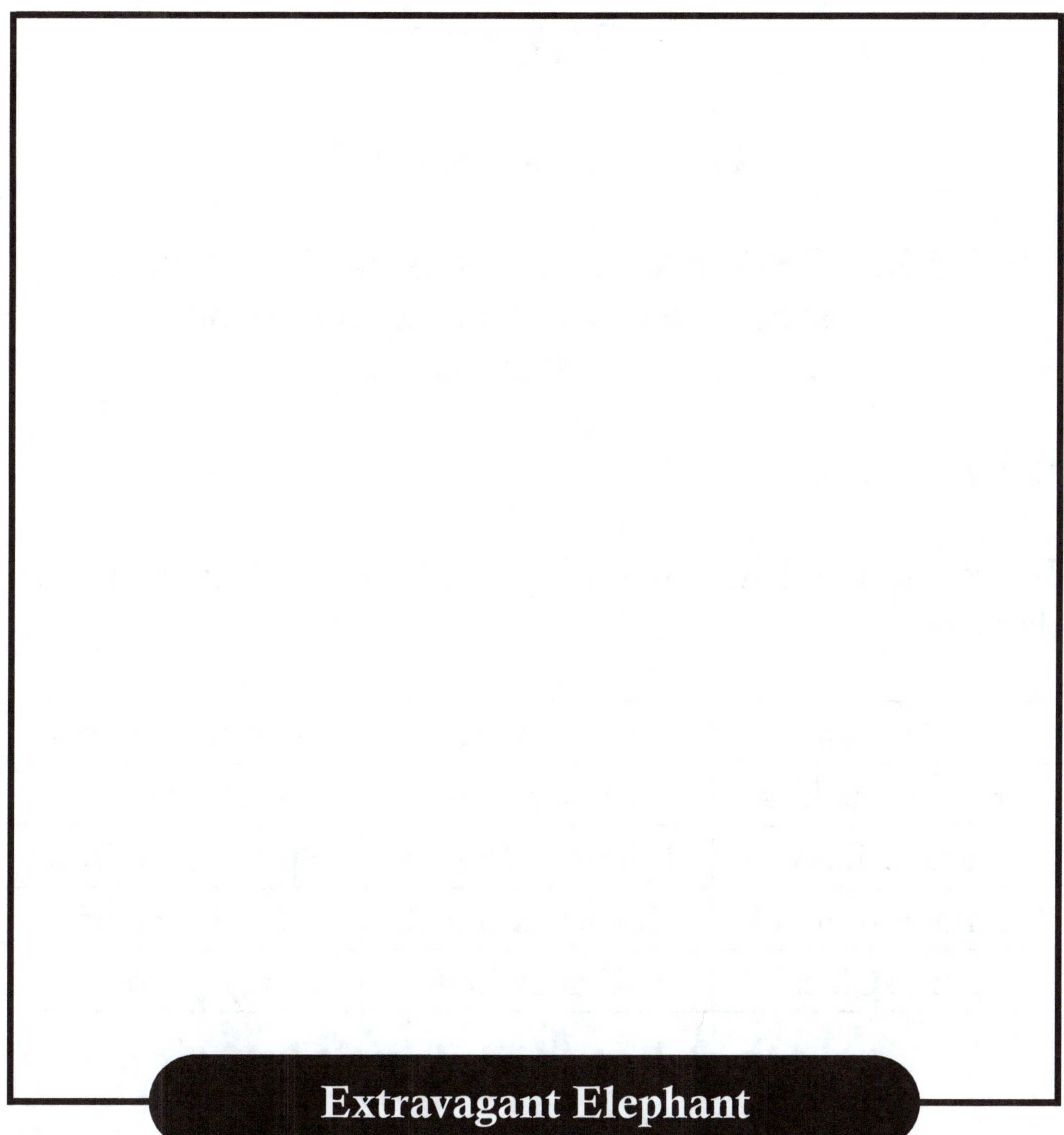

Extravagant Elephant

PROMPT 31

Overprotective Owl

The Task: Draw an owl that looks like it is about to send its teenage daughter out on her first date with a chicken hawk.

Required Objects:

Incorporate at least three of the following items into your drawing.

Shotgun	First Aid Kit	Security Camera
Brass Knuckles	Sex Ed Book	GPS Device
Radar Dish	Infrared Googles	Bullet Proof Vest
Ammunition Belt	Torture Manual	Lie Detector
Large Clock	Chasity Belt	Empty Coffin

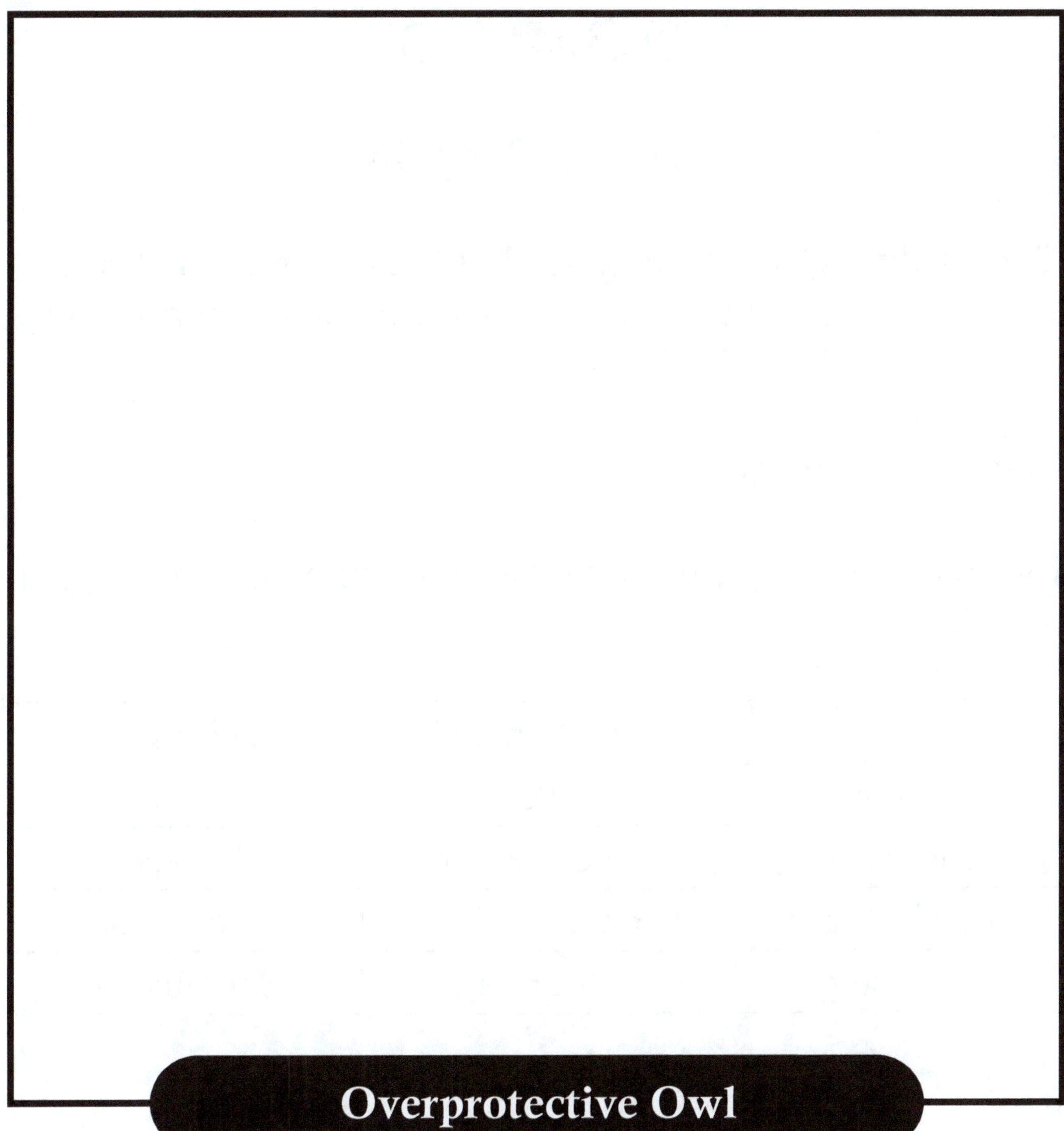

Overprotective Owl

PROMPT 32

Parched Penguin

The Task: Draw a penguin that looks like it has spent the past week in the desert without a single ice cube for miles.

Required Objects:

Incorporate at least three of the following items into your drawing.

Cactus	Tumbleweed	Bull Skull
Sand Dunes	North Pole Sign	Sun
Empty Bottle	Ice Cube Tray	Mirage
Pretzel Stand	Cinnamon Bottle	Weetabix Box
Toaster	Flour Bag	Salt Shaker

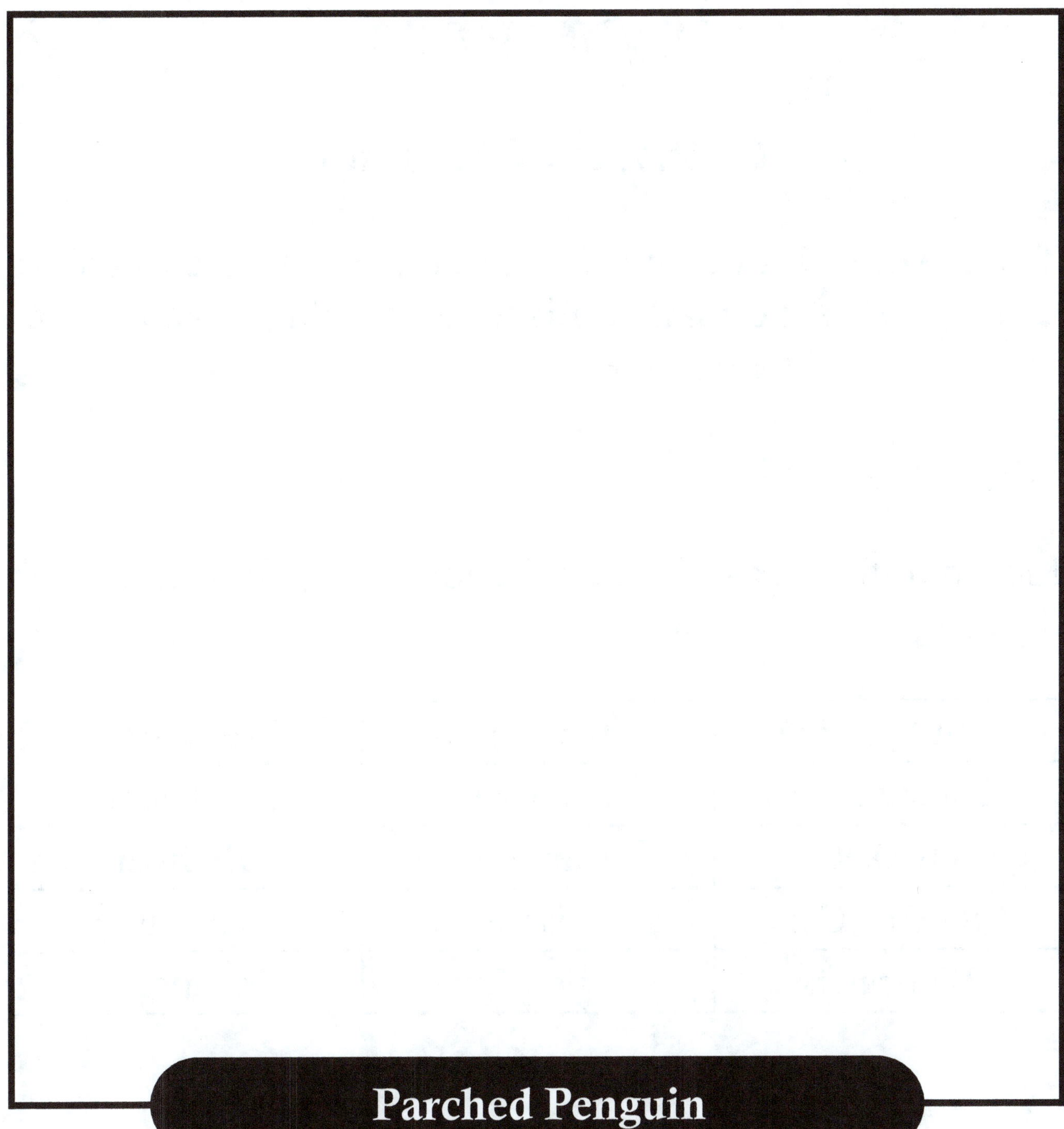

Parched Penguin

PROMPT 33

Captivated Chipmunk

The Task: Draw a chipmunk that has just discovered a supermarket mixed nut vending machine for the first time.

Required Objects:

Incorporate at least three of the following items into your drawing.

Nut Machine	Empty Coin Purse	Eye Glasses
Floating Hearts	A Nickel	Step Ladder
Basket	Hammer	Out Of Order Sign
Climbing Gear	Tissue	Glass Cutter
Binoculars	Suction Cups	Trampoline

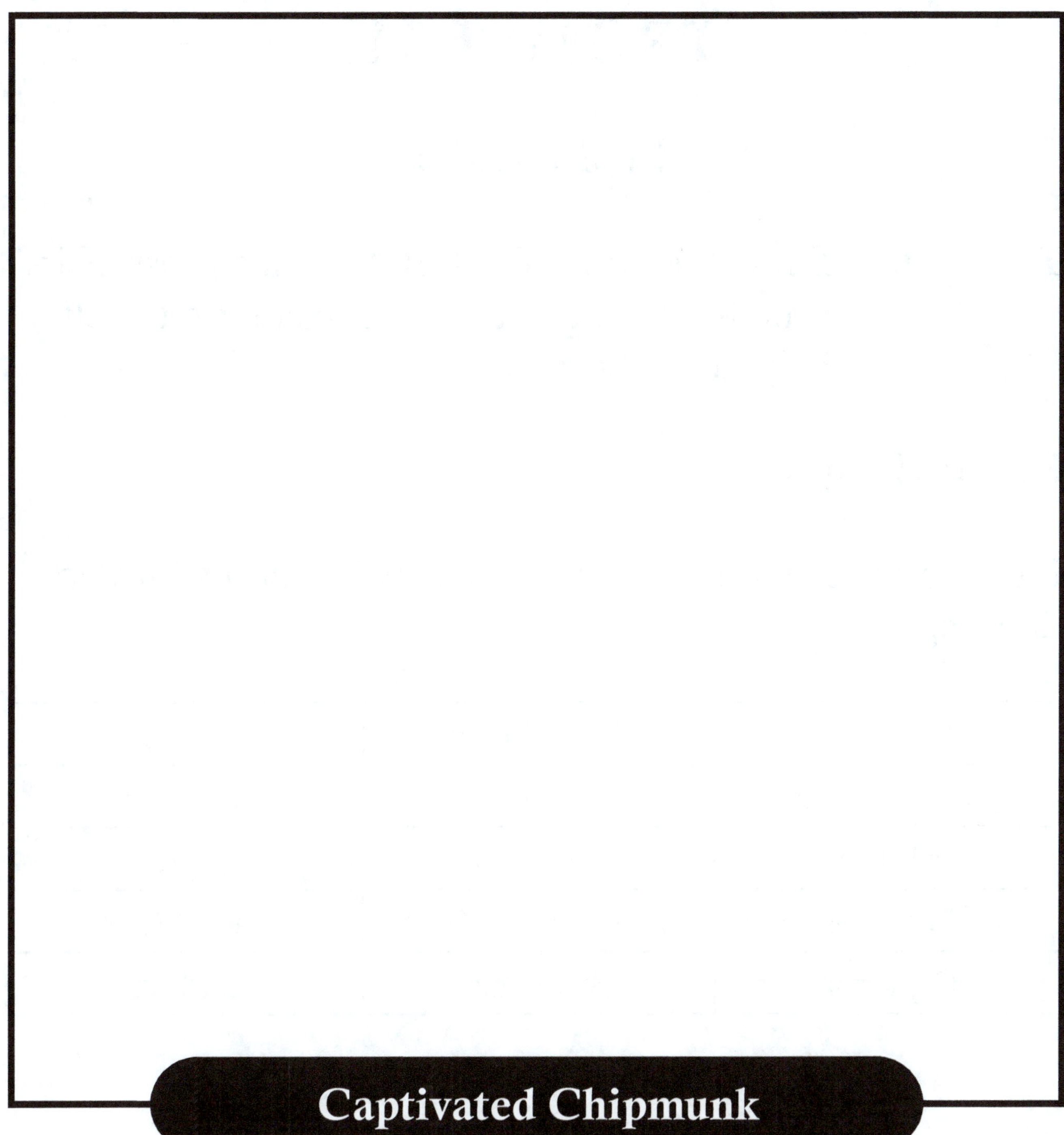

Captivated Chipmunk

PROMPT 34

Brilliant Bat

The Task: Draw the kind of bat that spends most of its time hanging upside down listening to self help audio books.

Required Objects:

Incorporate at least three of the following items into your drawing.

iPod	Headphones	Chair
Bookshelves	Books	Eyeglasses
Desk Lamp	Table	Laptop
Chalkboard	Graduation Cap	Report Card
Diploma	Briefcase	Ladder

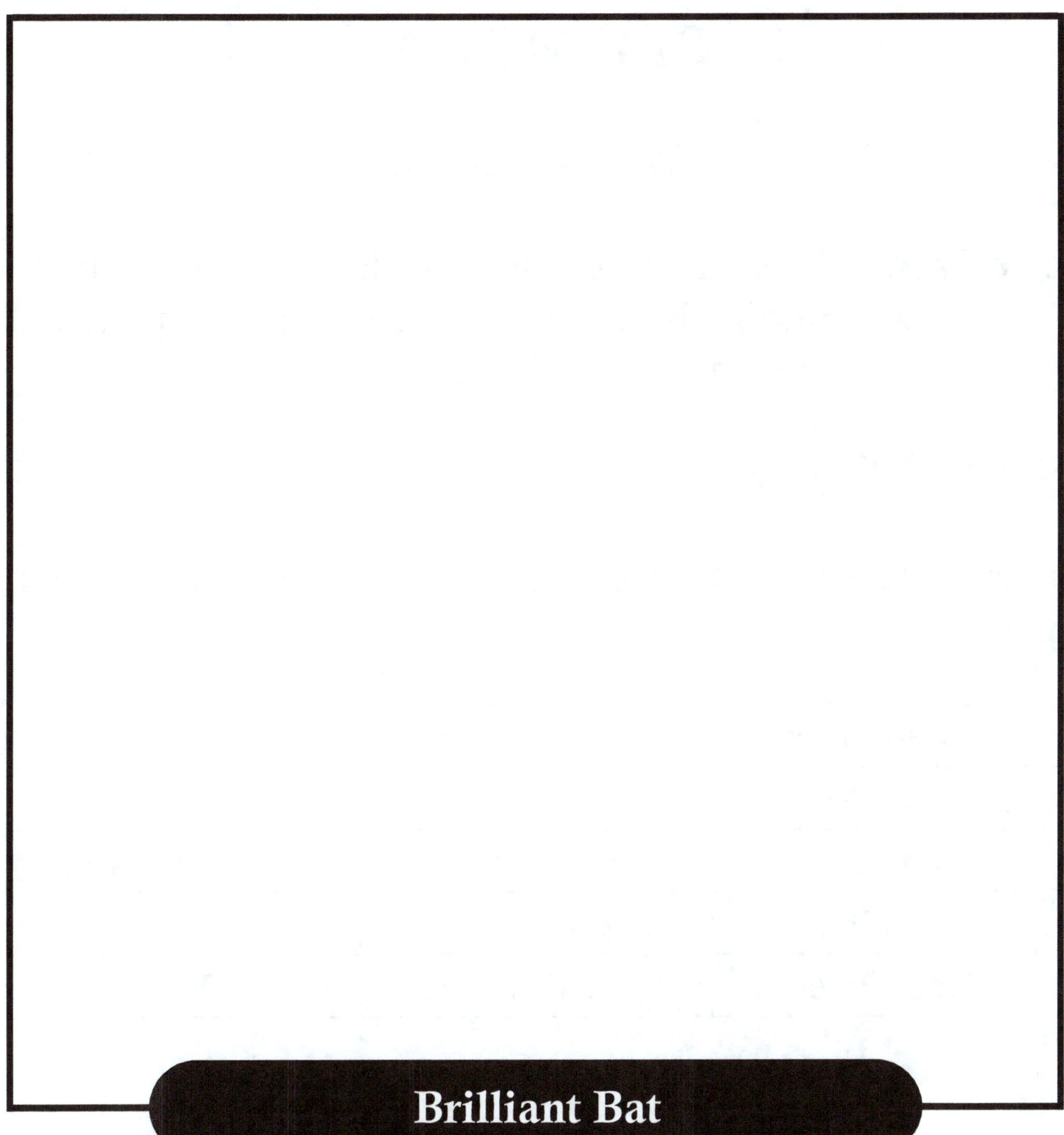

Brilliant Bat

PROMPT 35

Dainty Dragon

The Task: Draw a dragon that would be much happier raiding little girls jewelery boxes rather than burning down villages.

Required Objects:

Incorporate at least three of the following items into your drawing.

Jewelry Box	Assorted Jewelry	Purse
Compact Mirror	Wig	Fake Eyelashes
Perfume Bottle	Hair Brush	Vanity Dresser
Doll	Lipstick Tube	Tiara
Hair Dryer	Stuffed Animal	Dress

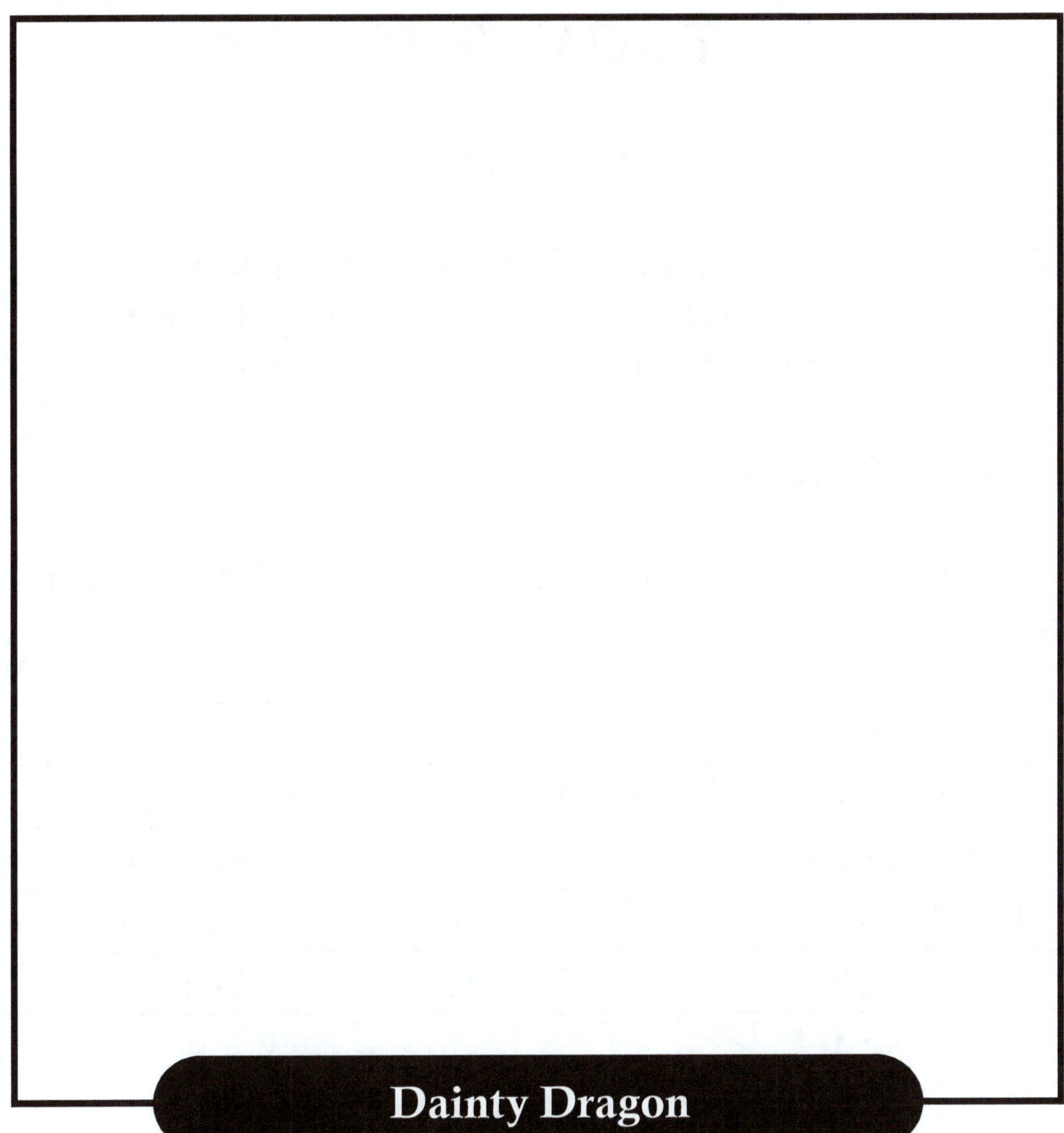

Dainty Dragon

PROMPT 36

Testy Turtle

The Task: Draw a turtle that has the temperament of an eighty year old man yelling at kids for riding their bikes across his lawn.

Required Objects:

Incorporate at least three of the following items into your drawing.

False Teeth	Eyeglasses	Walker
BP Monitor	Adult Diaper	Rocking Chair
Wheel Chair	Slippers	Blanket
Hot Water Bottle	Tissue Box	Bingo Card
Rolling Pin	Ear Trumpet	IV Bag

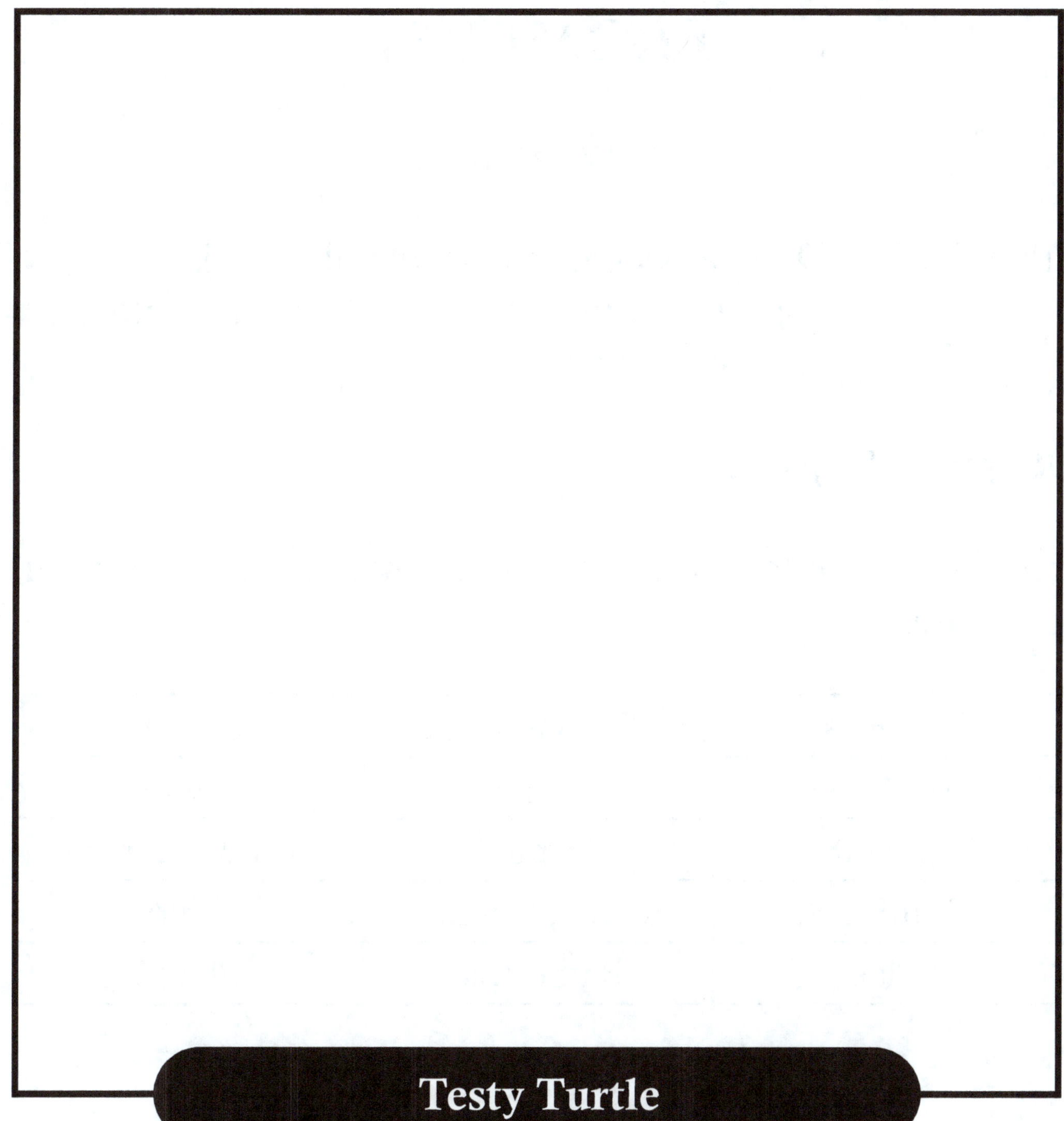

Testy Turtle

PROMPT 37

Brave Beagle

The Task: Draw a beagle that seems like the kind of dog that would run into a burning building to save puppies.

Required Objects:

Incorporate at least three of the following items into your drawing.

Fire Hose	Fireman Gear	Ladder
Eye Mask	Cape	Tights
Sword	Armour	Bow and Arrow
Utility Belt	Viking Helmet	Kilt
Flag	Battle Axe	Shield

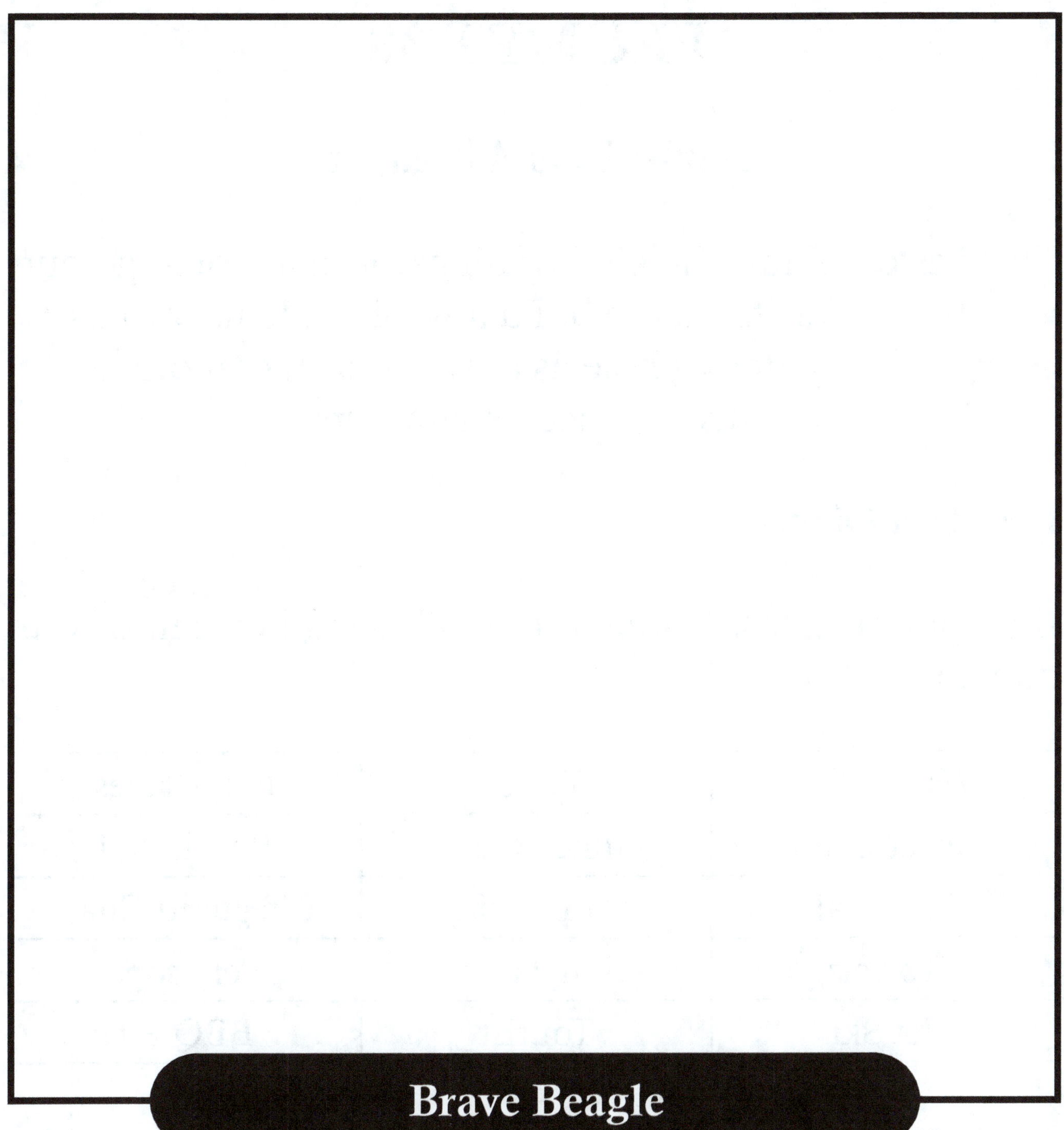

Brave Beagle

PROMPT 38

Ambitious Alligator

The Task: Draw the kind of alligator that would go out of its way to build a water slide next to its watering hole as a way to attract more victims … I mean swimmers.

Required Objects:

Incorporate at least three of the following items into your drawing.

Water Slide	Pond	Palm Trees
Ticket Booth	Inner Tube	Beach Ball
Sun Chair	Umbrella	Lifeguard Chair
Towels	Sunglasses	Periscope
Jet Ski	Tourist	BBQ Pit

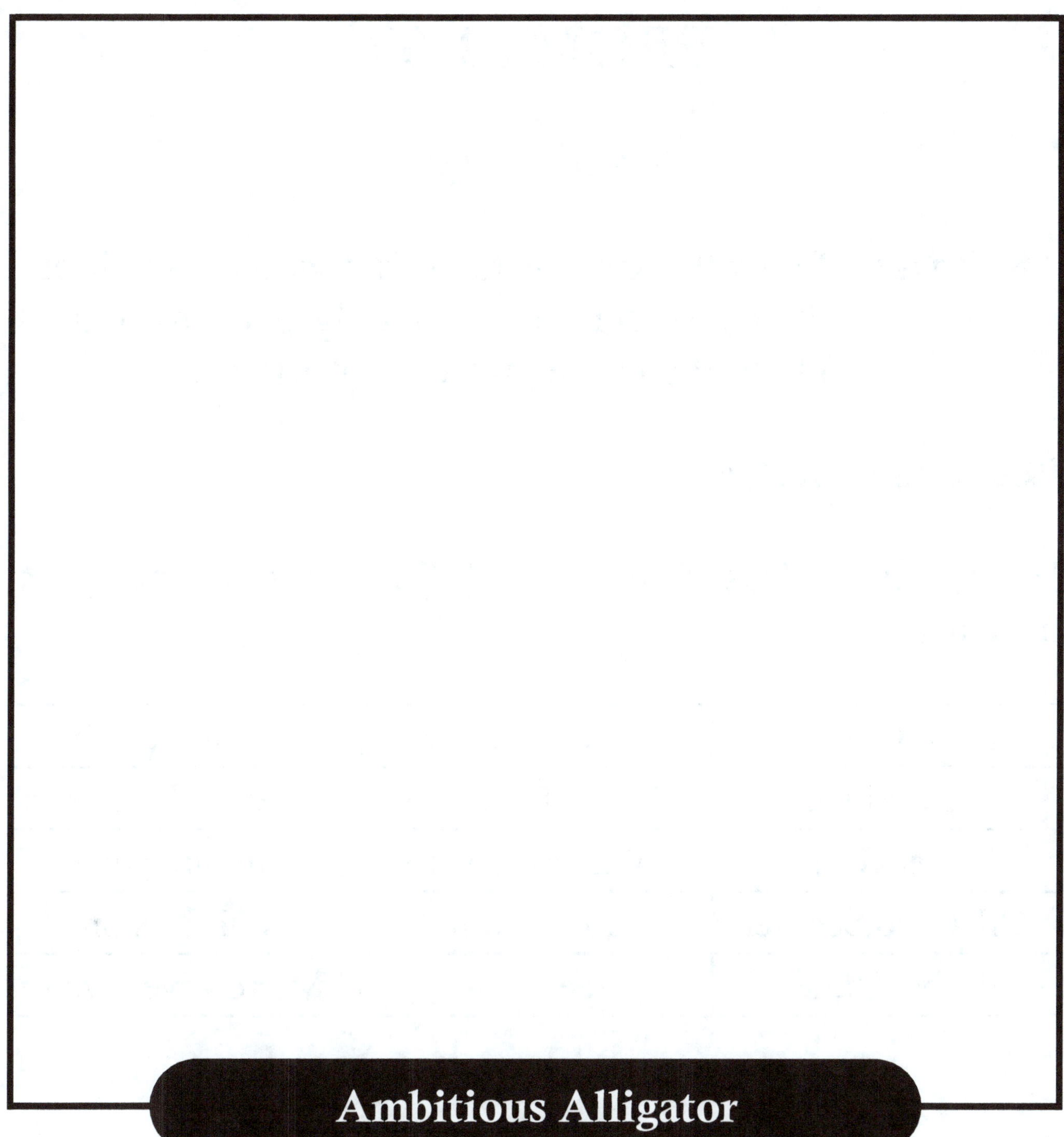

Ambitious Alligator

PROMPT 39

Techie Tiger

The Task: Draw the kind of tiger that would use all of the latest technological gadgets to make its life in the jungle more comfortable.

Required Objects:

Incorporate at least three of the following items into your drawing.

Laptop Computer	Big Screen TV	Air Conditioning
Fish Finder	Pocket Protector	Nerdy Glasses
Net Gun	Water Cooler	Satellite Dish
Off Road Scooter	Taser Gun	Night Vision
Robot Butler	Tree House	Microwave Oven

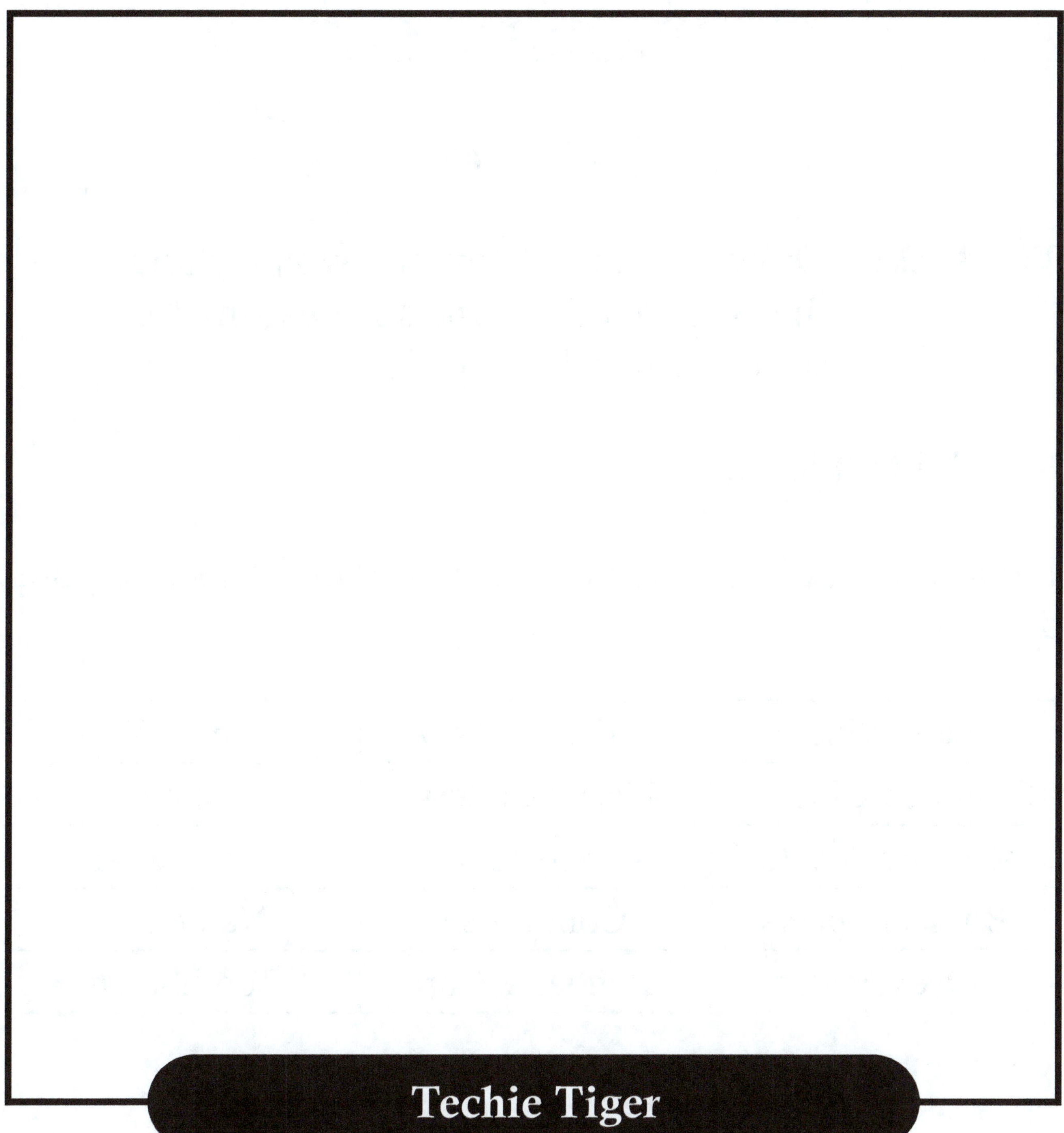
Techie Tiger

PROMPT 40

Flaky Fox

The Task: Draw the kind of fox that would stand by the chicken coupe window waiting for someone to take its order.

Required Objects:

Incorporate at least three of the following items into your drawing.

Coupe Window	Cafeteria Tray	Paper Bib
Confused Chicken	Plastic Cutlery	Coupons
Mobility Scooter	Party Hat	Underwear
Bunny Slippers	Coin Purse	Name Tag
Oven Mitts	Refillable Cup	Toothbrush

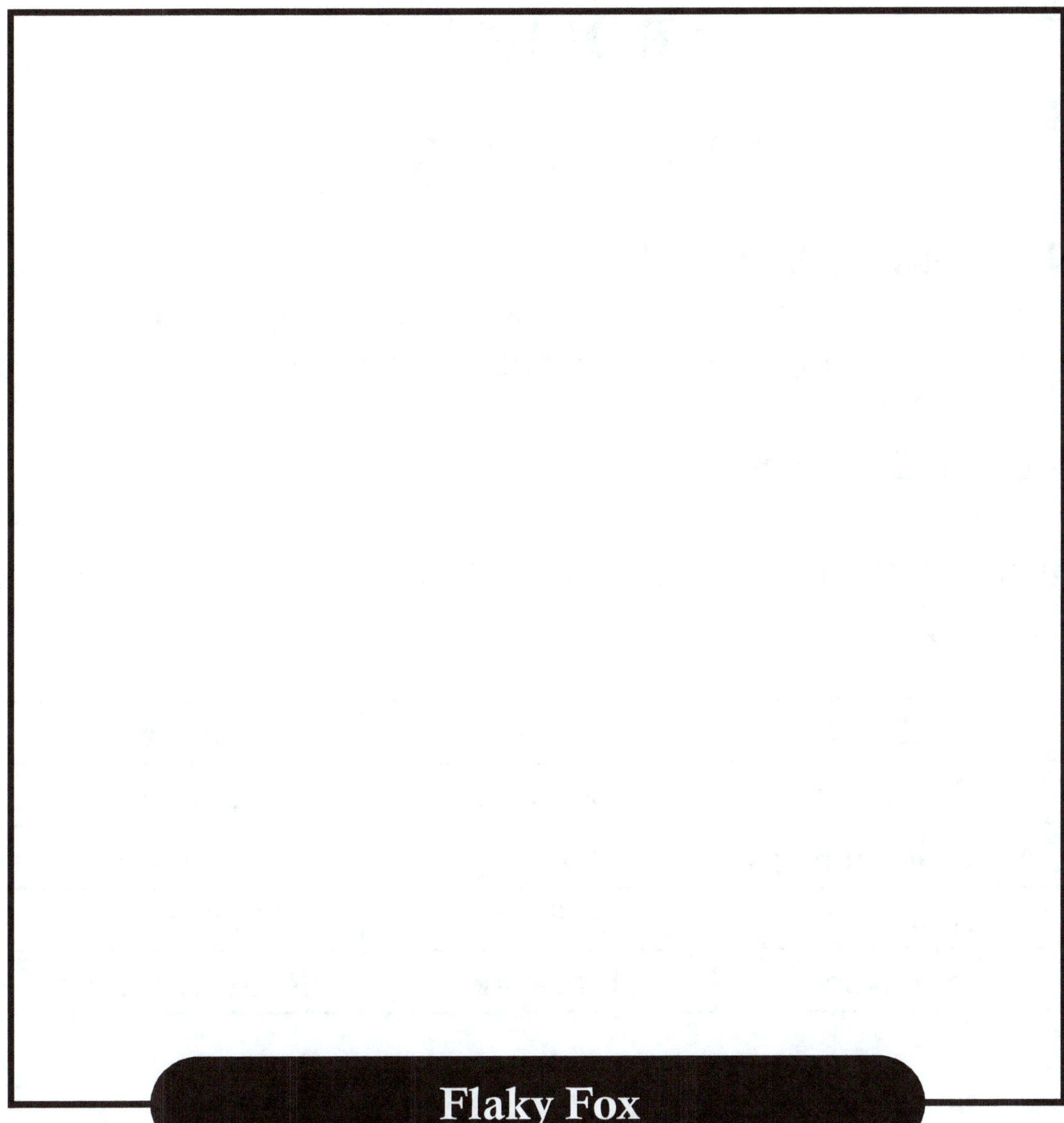

Flaky Fox

PROMPT 41

Boisterous Buffalo

The Task: Draw the kind of buffalo that would paint a target on its butt and then jump up and down taunting approaching hunters.

Required Objects:

Incorporate at least three of the following items into your drawing.

Paint Brush	Paint Can	Bullhorn
Clown Wig	Billboard	Neon Sign
Directional Flags	Tutu	Dart Board
Spot Lights	Balloons	Microphone
Speakers	Fireworks	Runway Lights

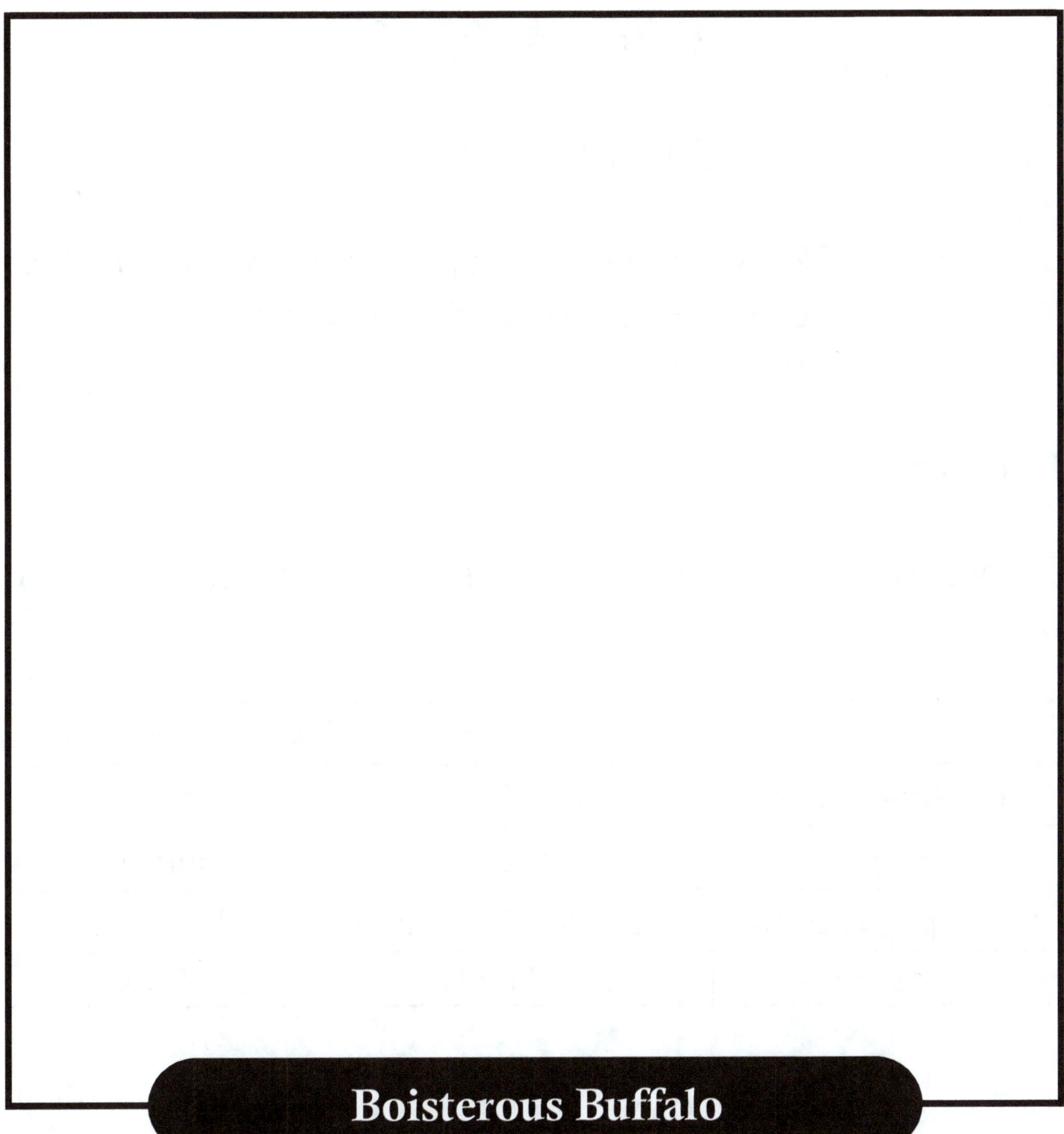

Boisterous Buffalo

PROMPT 42

Charming Coyote

The Task: Draw the type of coyote that is so irresistibly cordial even the roadrunners swoon in its presence.

Required Objects:

Incorporate at least three of the following items into your drawing.

Ascot Tie	Flower Bouquet	Box of Chocolates
Perfume Bottle	Top Hat	Cane
Cape	Gloves	Monocle
Champagne Bottle	Wrapped Present	Teddy Bear
Candles	Rose Petals	Lapel Flower

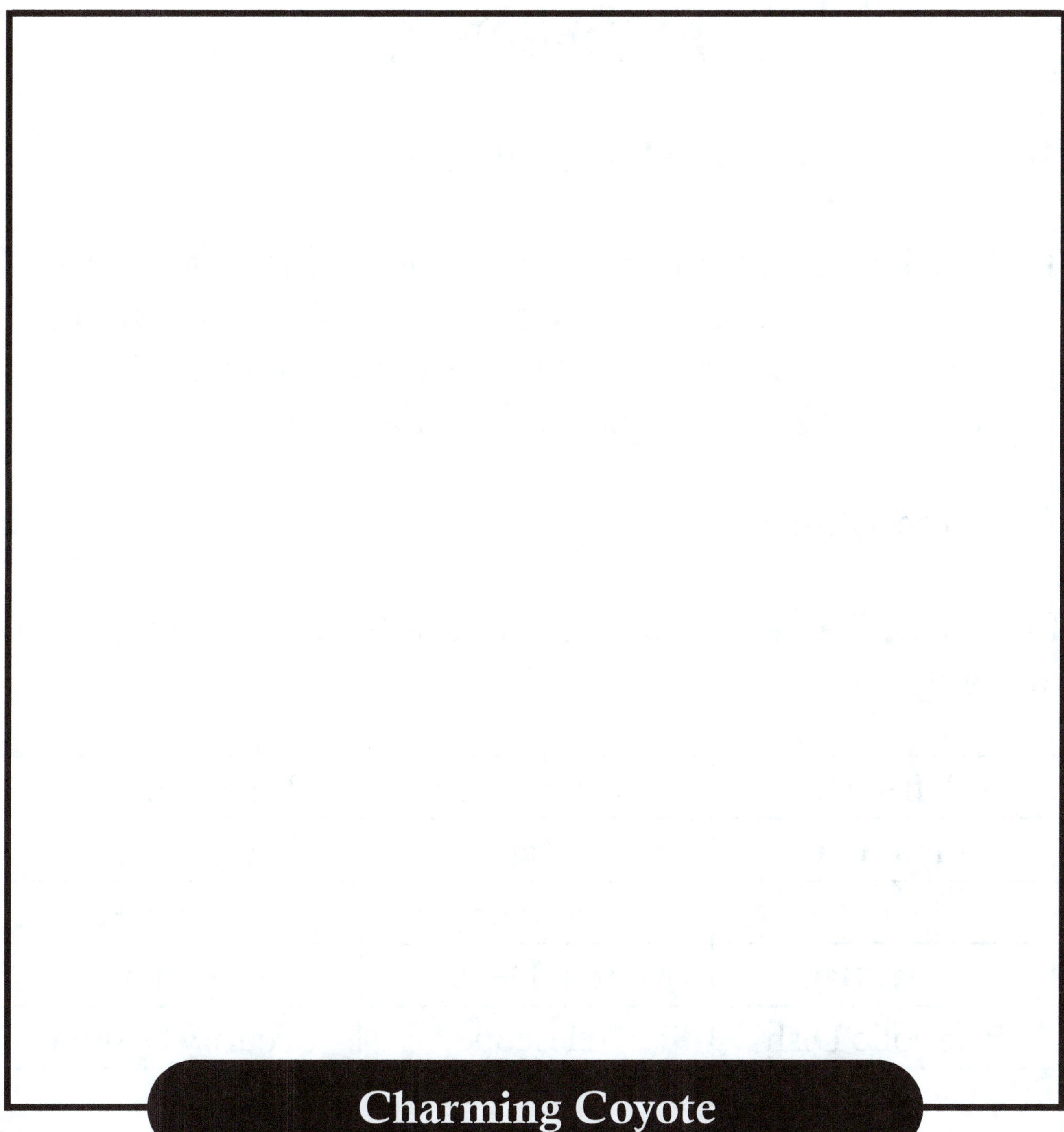

Charming Coyote

PROMPT 43

Alert Anteater

The Task: Draw an anteater that is so attentive it can discern the footsteps of every single ant for miles around. Unfortunately, having this ability is kind of freaking it out.

Required Objects:

Incorporate at least three of the following items into your drawing.

Coffee Pot	Stethoscope	Energy Drink
Radar Gun	Map	Drawing Board
Cigarettes	Ash Tray	Toothpicks
Sugar Bag	Motion Detector	Headphones
Parabolic Dish	Telescope	Security System

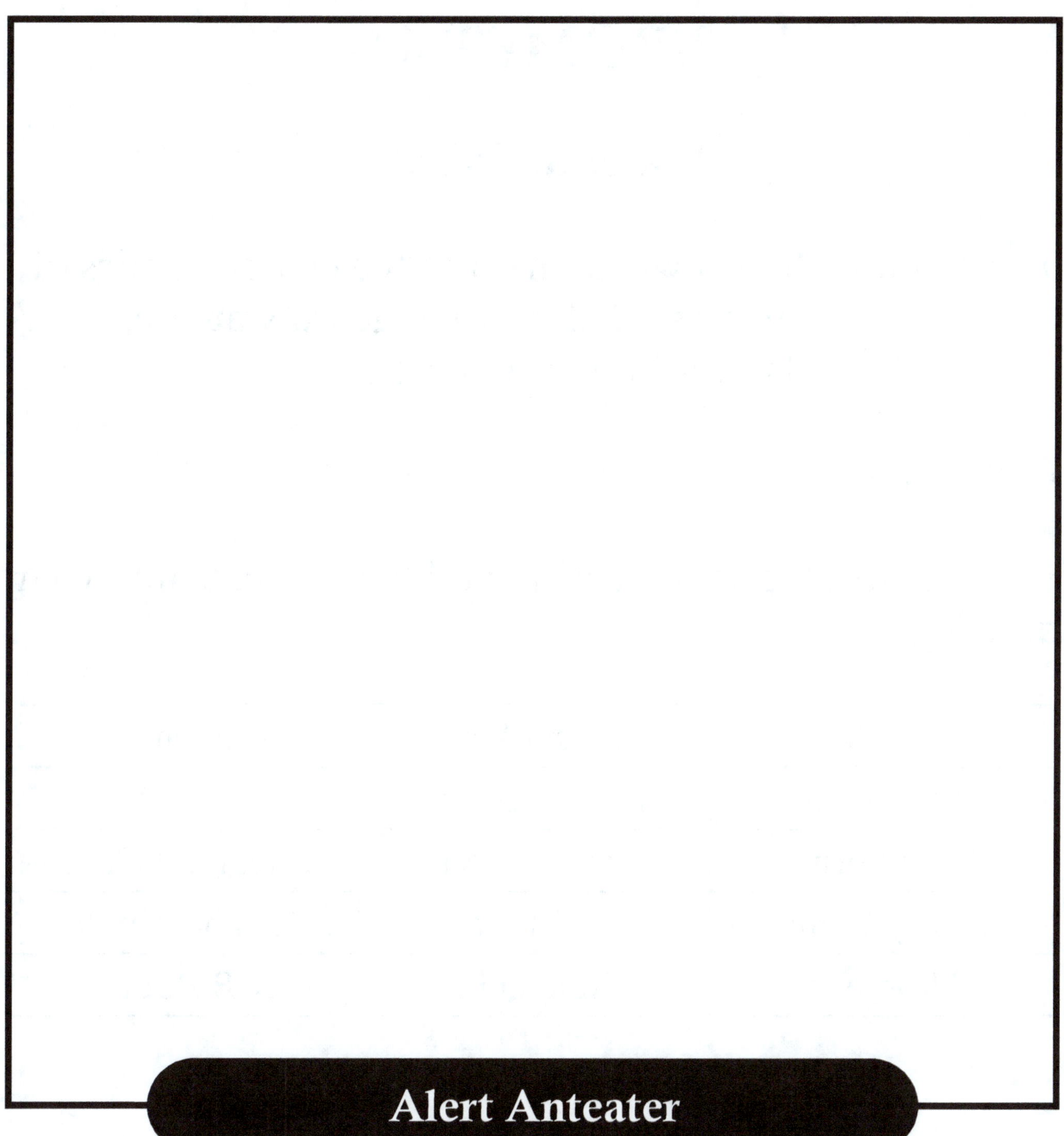

Alert Anteater

PROMPT 44

Watchful Whale

The Task: Draw a whale that has the characteristics of a grade school crossing guard watching over a large school of guppies.

Required Objects:

Incorporate at least three of the following items into your drawing.

Stop Sign	Safety Vest	Binoculars
Flashlight	Life Preserver	Whistle
Bullhorn	First Aid Kit	Lifeguard Chair
Security Camera	Lunch Pail	Portable Cooler
Umbrella	Handcuffs	CB Radio

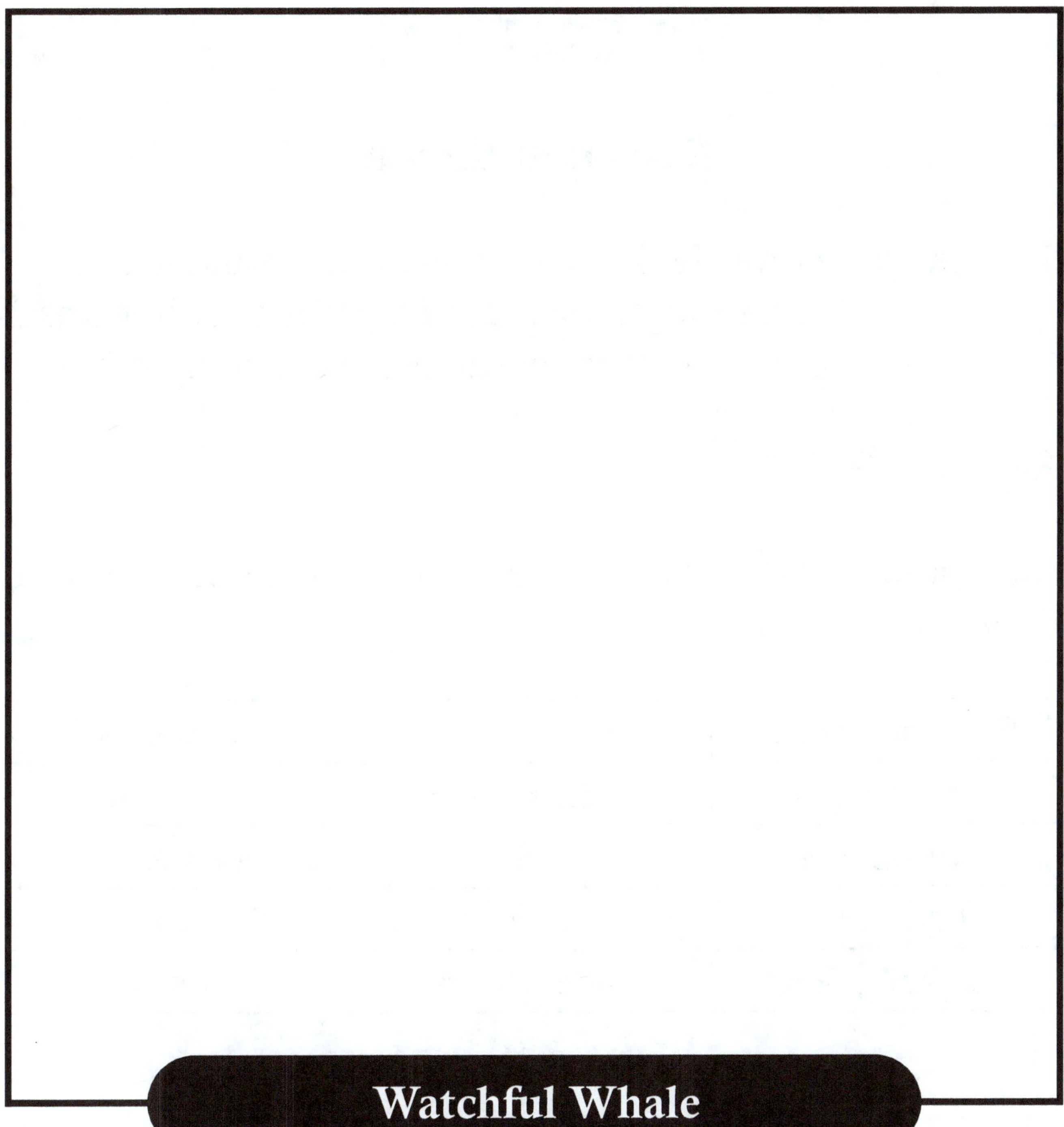

Watchful Whale

PROMPT 45

Reluctant Rabbit

The Task: Draw the kind of rabbit that would avoid eating vegetables from a garden until it was certain that no pesticides were being used.

Required Objects:

Incorporate at least three of the following items into your drawing.

Radiation Meter	Test Tubes	Microscope
Bunsen Burner	Glass Beaker	Lab Coat
Poison Sign	Caution Tape	Garden
Pesticide Sprayer	Gas Mask	Hard Hat
Hazmat Suit	Shoe Covers	Tongs

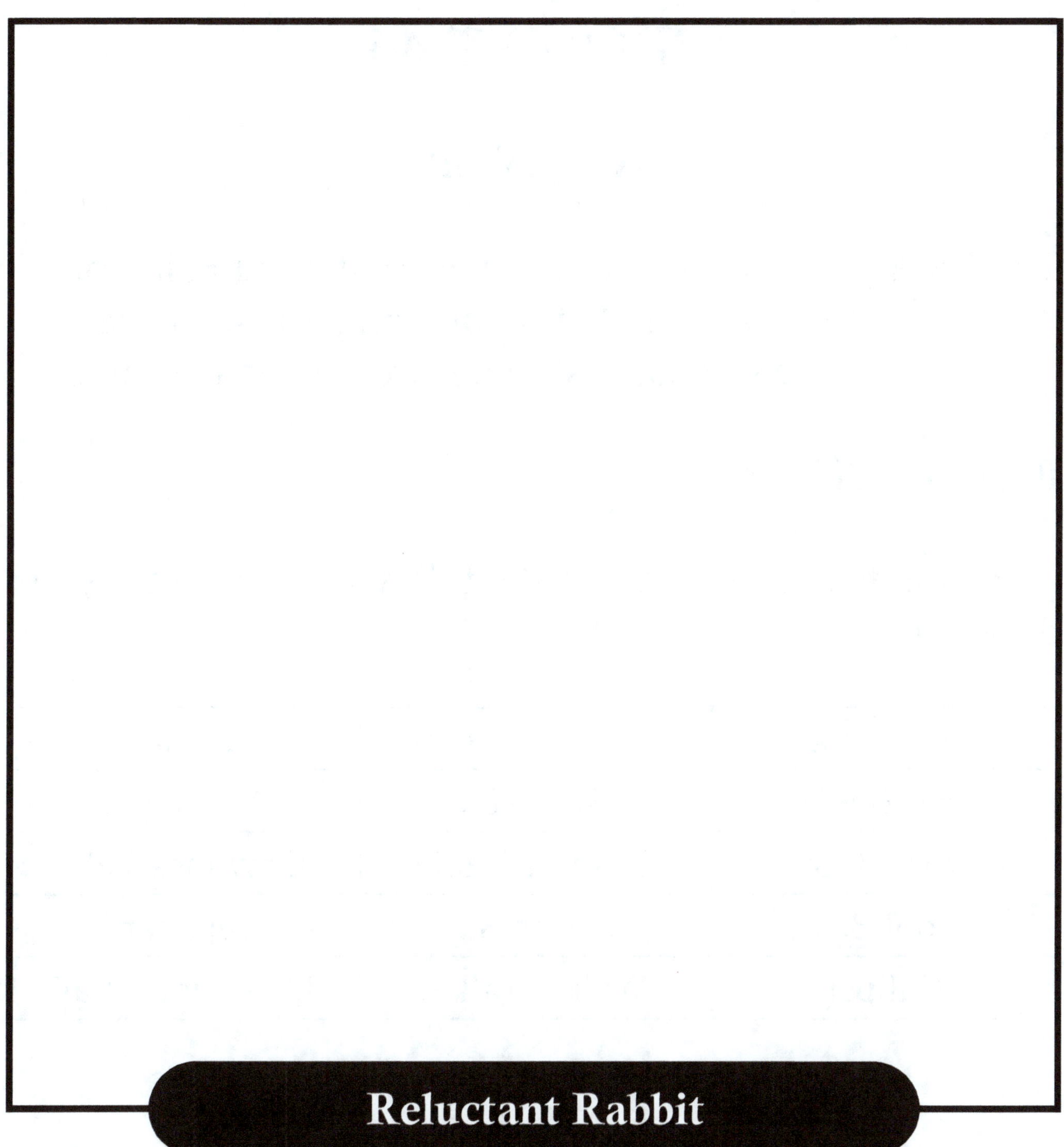
Reluctant Rabbit

PROMPT 46

Wary Wolf

The Task: Draw the kind of wolf that would plan out every detail before blowing down a little pig's house just to ensure no one got hurt.

Required Objects:

Incorporate at least three of the following items into your drawing.

Blue Prints	Measuring Tape	Calculator
Eye Glasses	Hard Hat	Notebook
Work Boots	Drafting Table	Drawings Tube
Tool Belt	Caution Sign	Clipboard
Caliper	Walkie Talkie	Demolition Ball

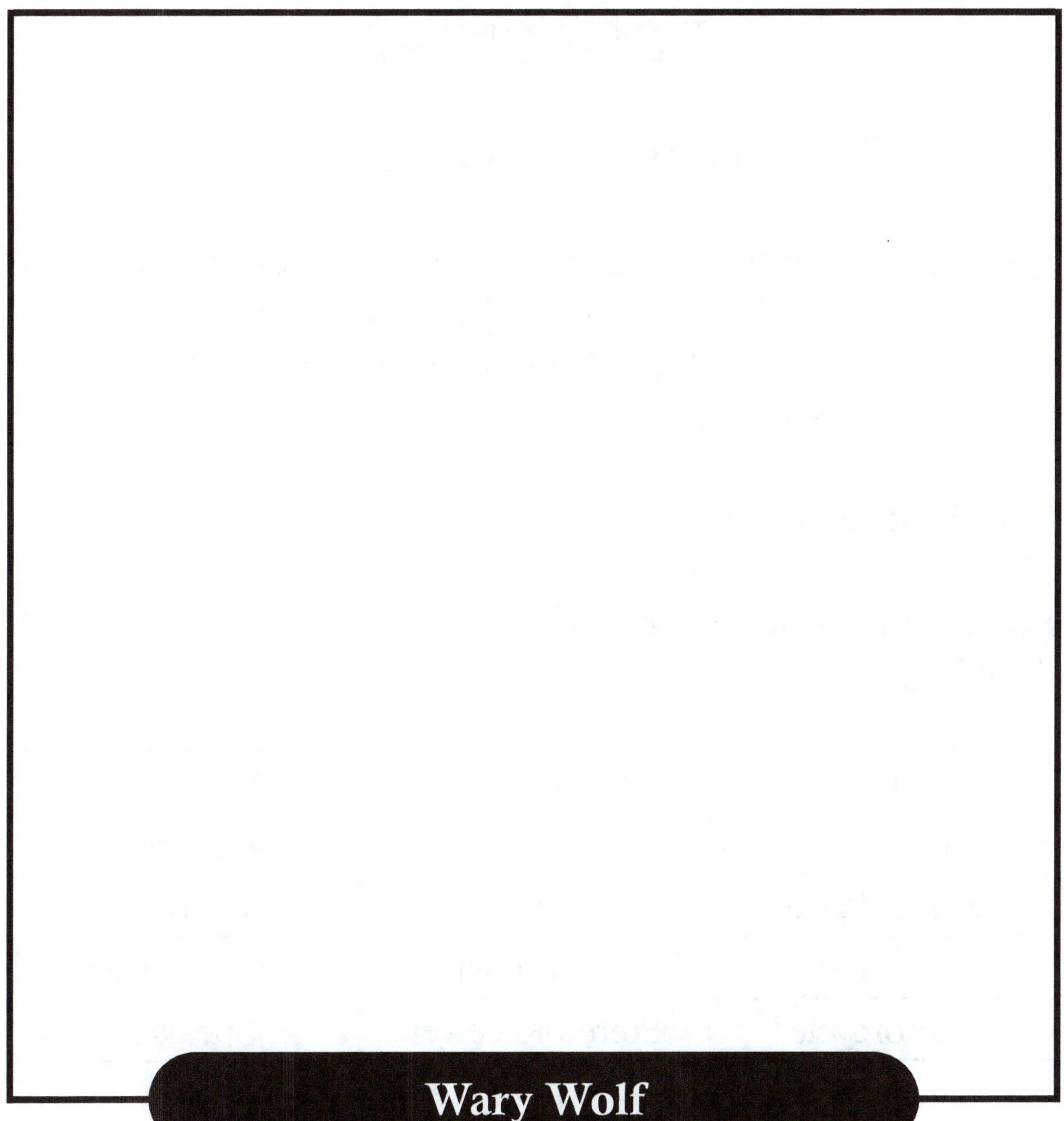

Wary Wolf

PROMPT 47

Demonic Dolphin

The Task: Draw the kind of dolphin that not only likes to flap its flippers, but also enjoys banging its head to a little death metal every now and then.

Required Objects:

Incorporate at least three of the following items into your drawing.

Tattoos	Mohawk Hair	Microphone
Slayer T-shirt	Devil Horns	Headphones
Skate Board	Flying V Guitar	Pentagram
Marshall Stack	Drum Set	Flame Thrower
Motorcycle	Stereo Receiver	Speakers

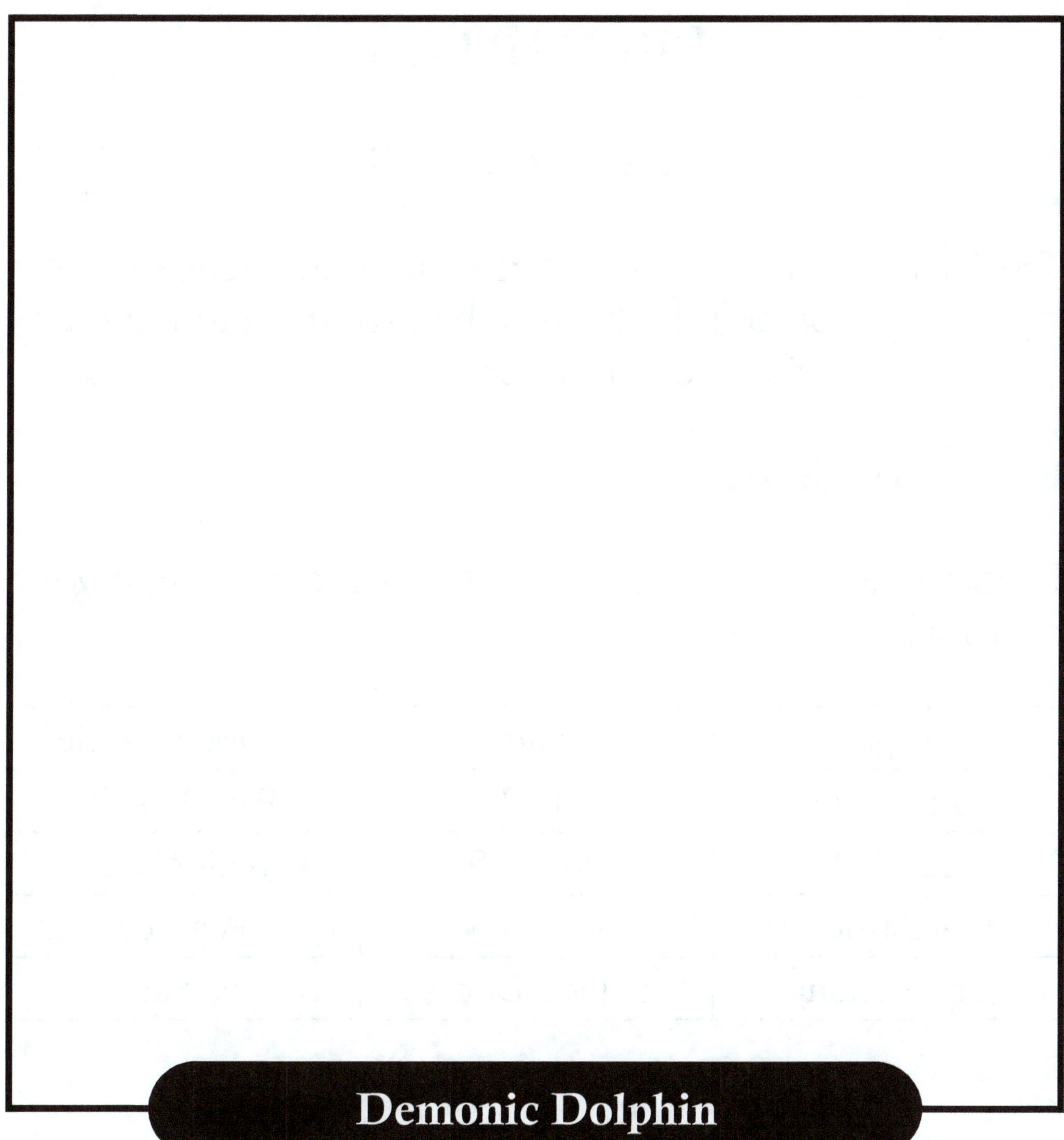

Demonic Dolphin

PROMPT 48

Belligerent Butterfly

The Task: Draw a butterfly that although delicate and beautiful, also has the extremely foul mouth of a drunken sailor.

Required Objects:

Incorporate at least three of the following items into your drawing.

Cigar	Tattoo	Whiskey Bottle
Bar Stool	Derby Hat	Park Bench
Jail Cell	Handcuffs	Sailor Hat
Tequila Bottle	Sombrero	Peg Leg
Street Lamp	Saloon Doors	Eye Patch

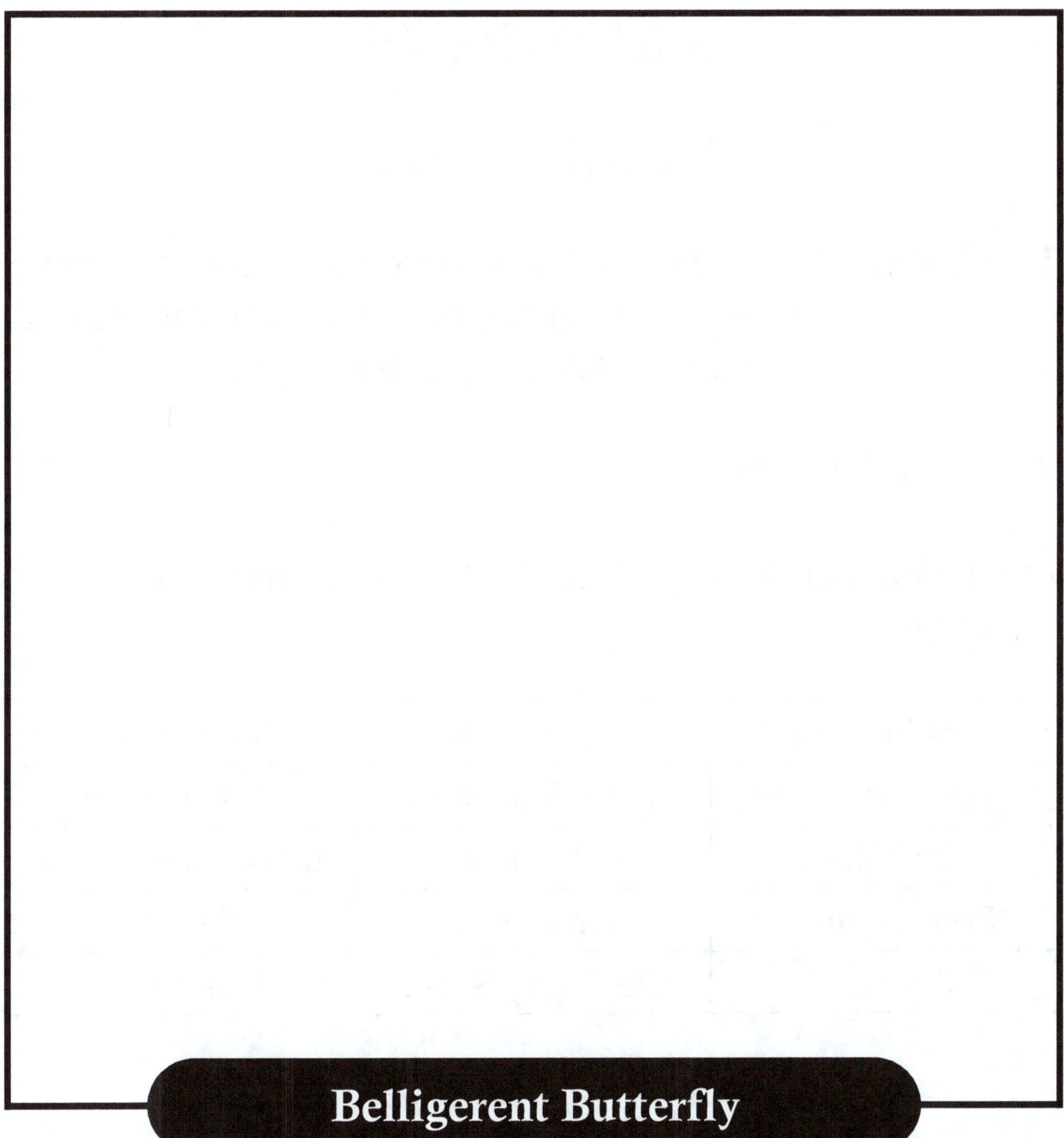

Belligerent Butterfly

PROMPT 49

Terrifying Turkey

The Task: Draw the kind of turkey that is so scary no one in their right mind would attempt to eat it for Thanksgiving dinner.

Required Objects:

Incorporate at least three of the following items into your drawing.

Gatling Gun	Bullet Belt	Bowie Knife
Hand Grenades	Brass Knuckles	Pickelhaube
Chain Saw	Machete	Missile Launcher
Body Armour	Crossbow	Barbed Wire
Fangs	Cranberry Sauce	Sunglasses

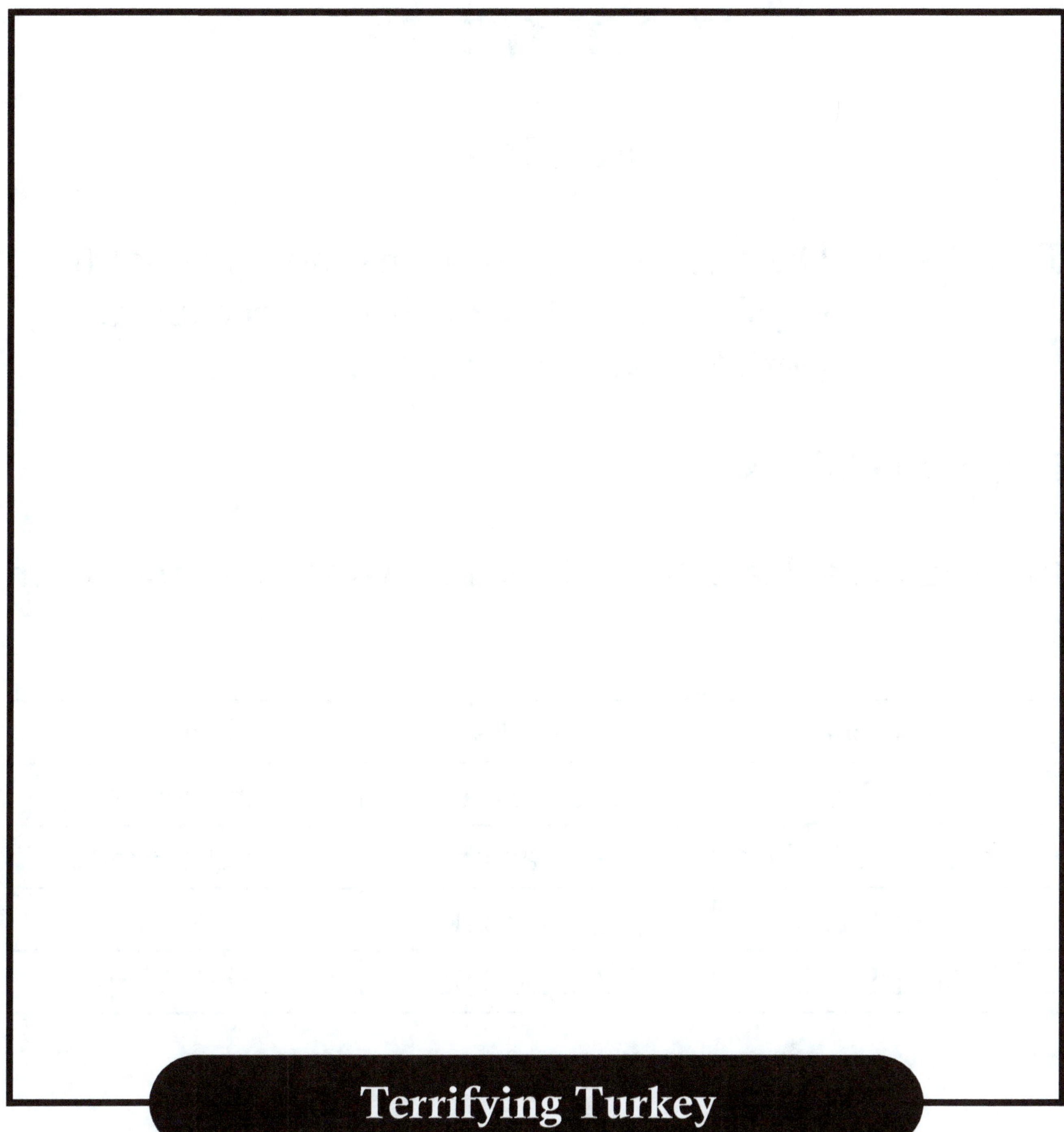

Terrifying Turkey

PROMPT 50

Buff Bear

The Task: Draw the kind of bear that not only has the physique, but also the drive to become the world's next Mr. Olympia.

Required Objects:

Incorporate at least three of the following items into your drawing.

Dumbbells	Barbells	Syringe
Protein Powder	Speedo Briefs	Refrigerator
Bucket of Chicken	Egg Cartons	Weight Bench
Trophies	Squat Rack	Towel
Water Bottle	Weight Belt	Wrist Wraps

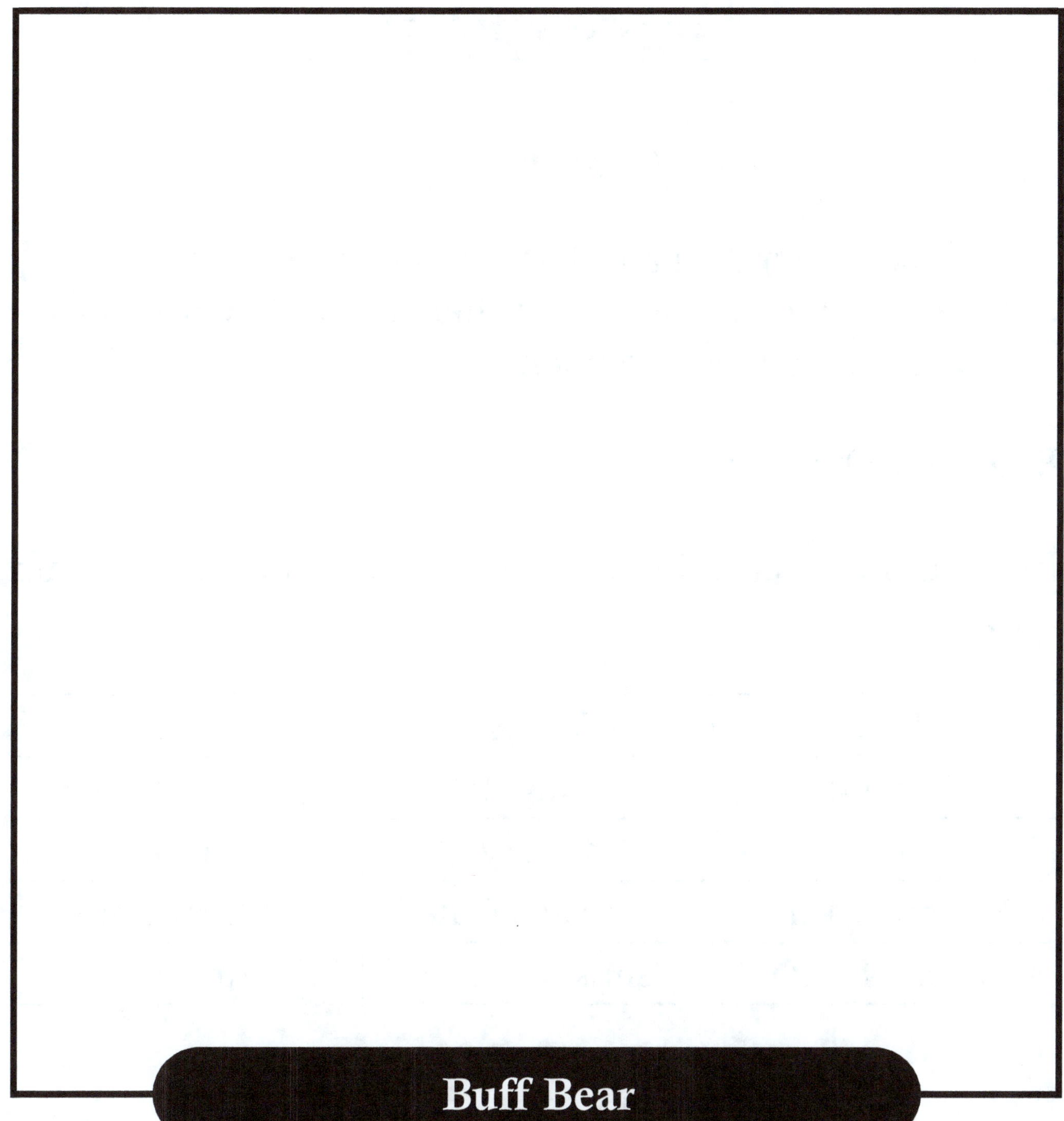

Buff Bear

PROMPT 51

Angelic Ant

The Task: Draw an ant that looks less like a sci-fi monster and more like a sparkly Christmas tree top ornament.

Required Objects:

Incorporate at least three of the following items into your drawing.

Halo	Wings	Harp
Trumpet	Flowing Robe	Magic Wand
Cloud	Rosary	Crucifix
Floating Hearts	Heaven's Gate	Reaper Scythe
Beams of Light	Christmas Tree	Ant Hill

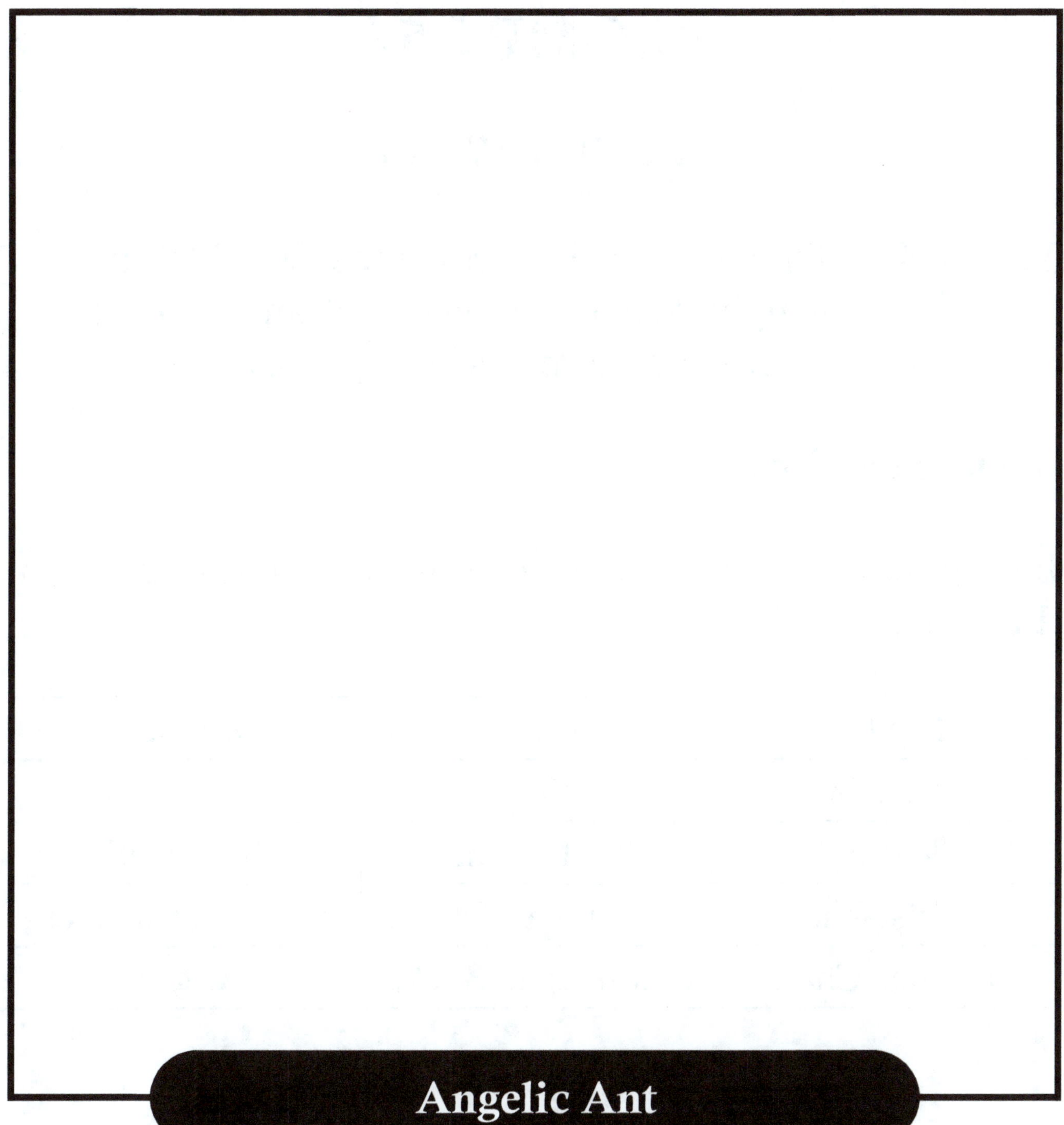

Angelic Ant

PROMPT 52

Wealthy Worm

The Task: Draw the kind of worm that wouldn't be caught dead crawling out of anything less than a premium priced organic apple.

Required Objects:

Incorporate at least three of the following items into your drawing.

Top Hat	Cane	Monocle
Dollar Bills	Apple Cart	Money Bags
Jewelry	Slot Machine	Bank Vault
Mustache	Private Jet	Stock Certificates
Lounge Chair	Champagne Bucket	Cigar

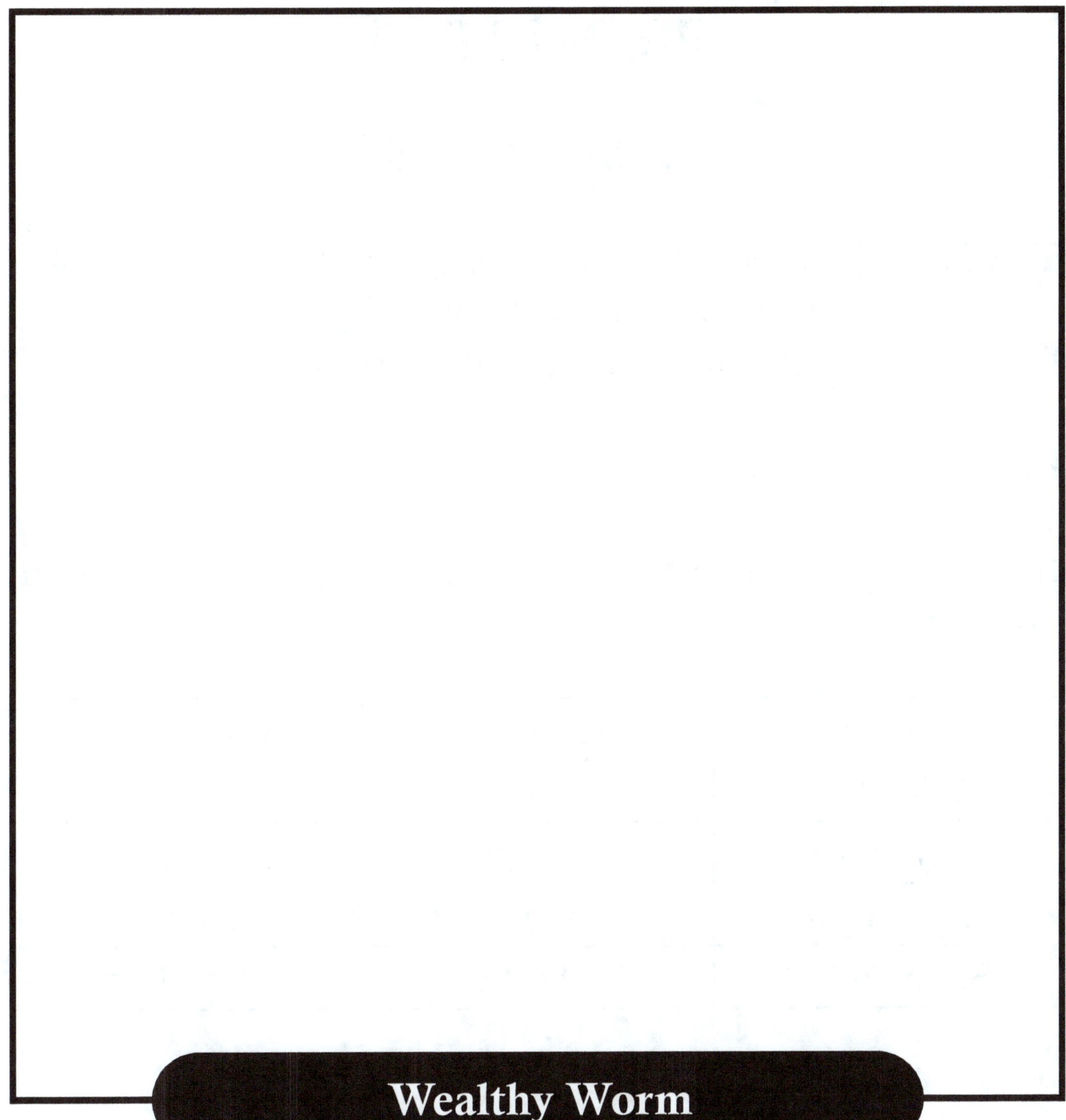

Wealthy Worm

PROMPT 53

Listless Lizard

The Task: Draw a lizard that is so lazy that instead of catching bugs as they fly by, just waits for them to drop dead of natural causes.

Required Objects:

Incorporate at least three of the following items into your drawing.

Pillow	Hammock	Sleep Mask
Flying Bugs	Plants	Tree Branch
Fly Paper	Bug Zapper	Bug Spray
Honey Jar	Rotting Fruit	Roach Motel
Butterfly Net	Light Bulb	Poop Pile

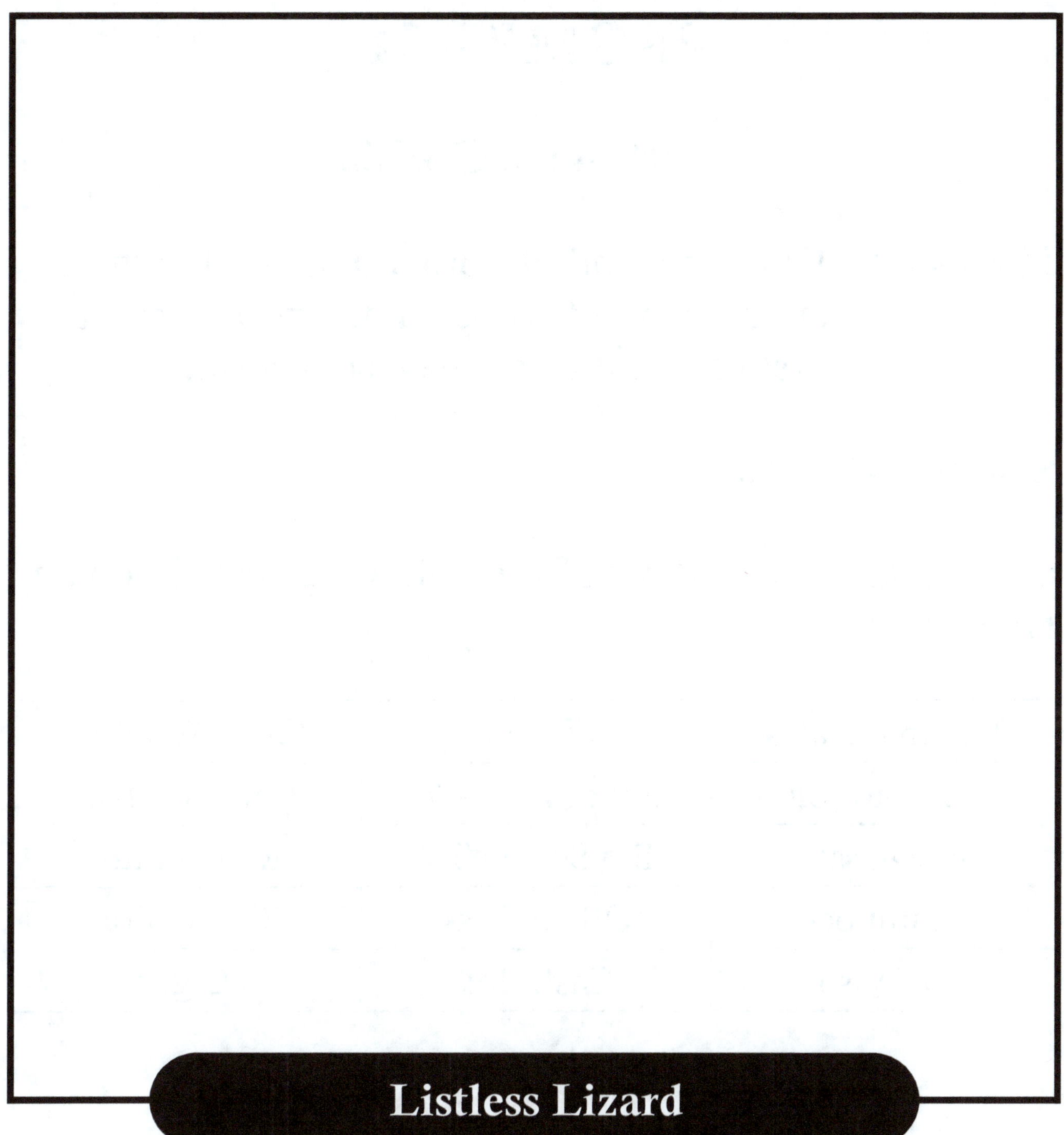

Listless Lizard

PROMPT 54

Gluttonous Gorilla

The Task: Draw the kind of gorilla that would refuse to come out of its pen at the zoo unless it first got a cut of the day's ticket sales.

Required Objects:

Incorporate at least three of the following items into your drawing.

Banana Crates	Wet Bar	Glass Window
No Photos Sign	Window Shades	Lounge Chair
Eyeglasses	Big Screen TV	Refrigerator
Hammock	Office Desk	Calculator
Sun Visor	Cash Box	Cigar

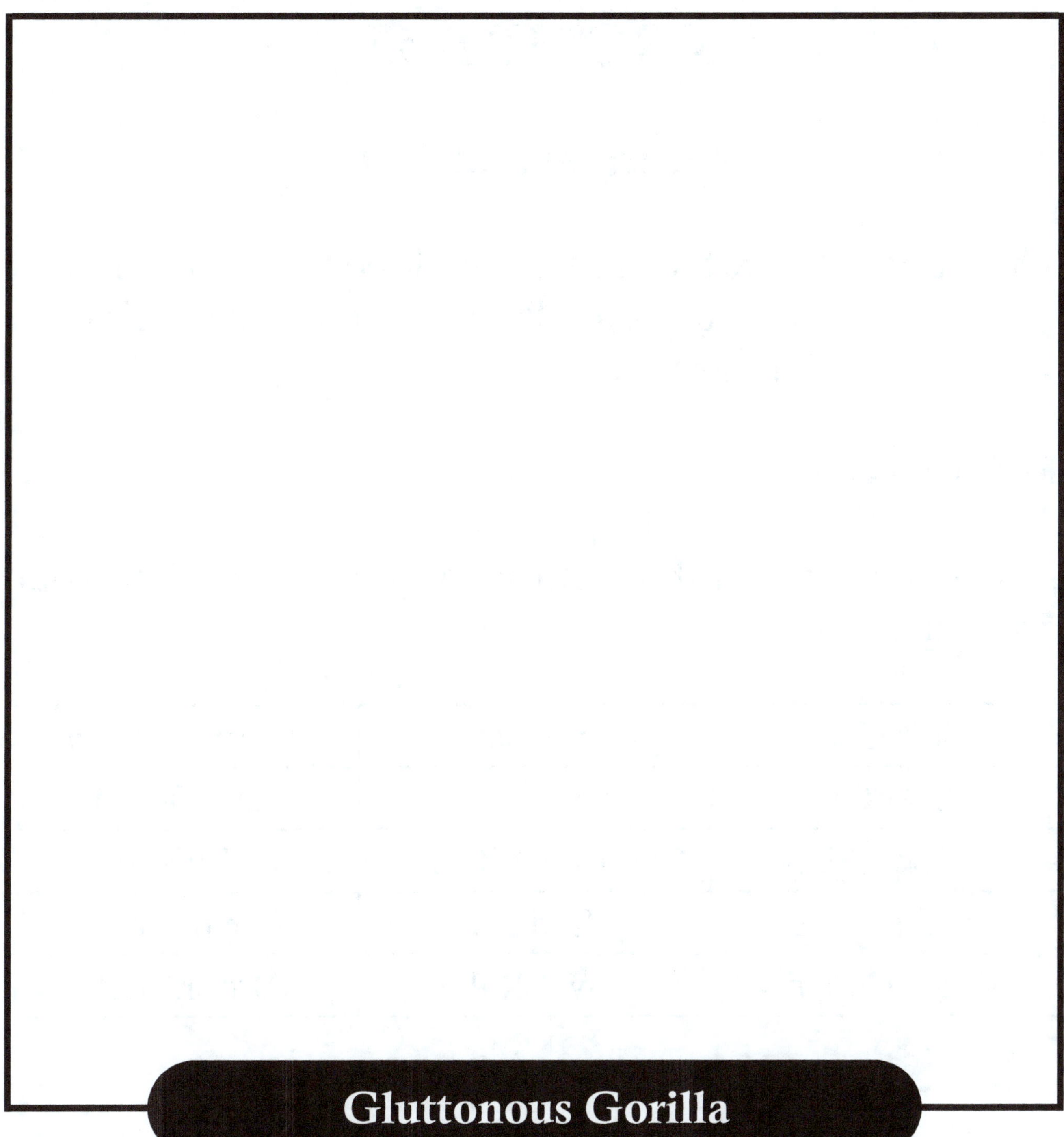
Gluttonous Gorilla

PROMPT 55

Assertive Antelope

The Task: Draw the kind of antelope that is so self assured it actually bosses the neighboring lions around.

Required Objects:

Incorporate at least three of the following items into your drawing.

Bull Horn	Police Baton	Leather Whip
Taser Gun	Wooden Stool	Clip Board
Pepper Spray	Police Uniform	Whistle
Safety Vest	Hard Hat	Lawnmower
Hedge Clippers	Lawn Rake	Broomstick

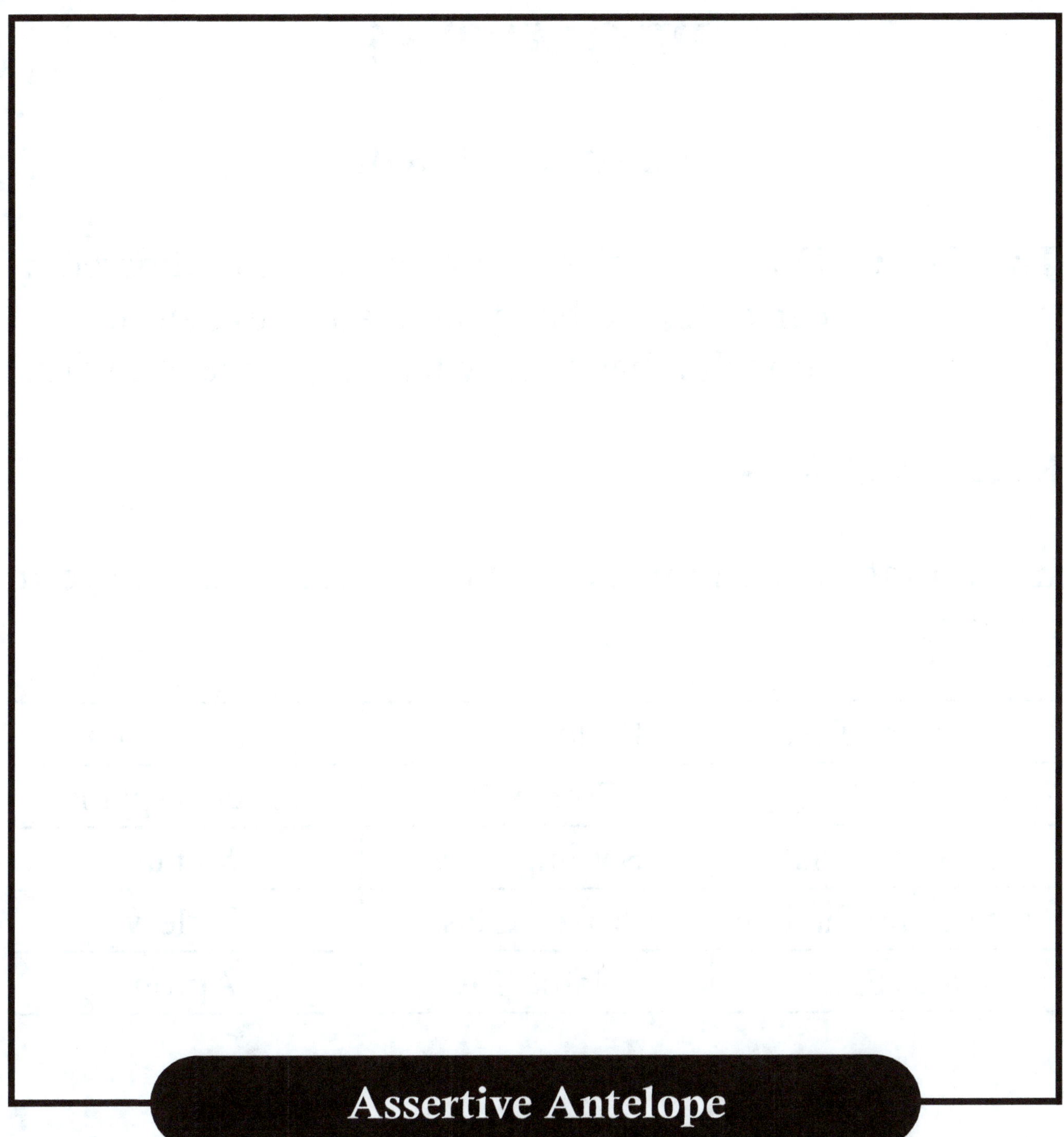# Assertive Antelope

PROMPT 56

Clumsy Centipede

The Task: Draw a centipede that is so uncoordinated it can't seem to hang on to anything, even though it has twenty hands to hang on with.

Required Objects:

Incorporate at least three of the following items into your drawing.

Banana Peel	Roller Skates	Elbow Pads
Book	Coffee Pot	Paper Napkins
Spaghetti Plate	Serving Tray	Menus
Ice Cream Sundae	Broken Glass	Cutlery
Water Pitcher	Name Tag	Apron

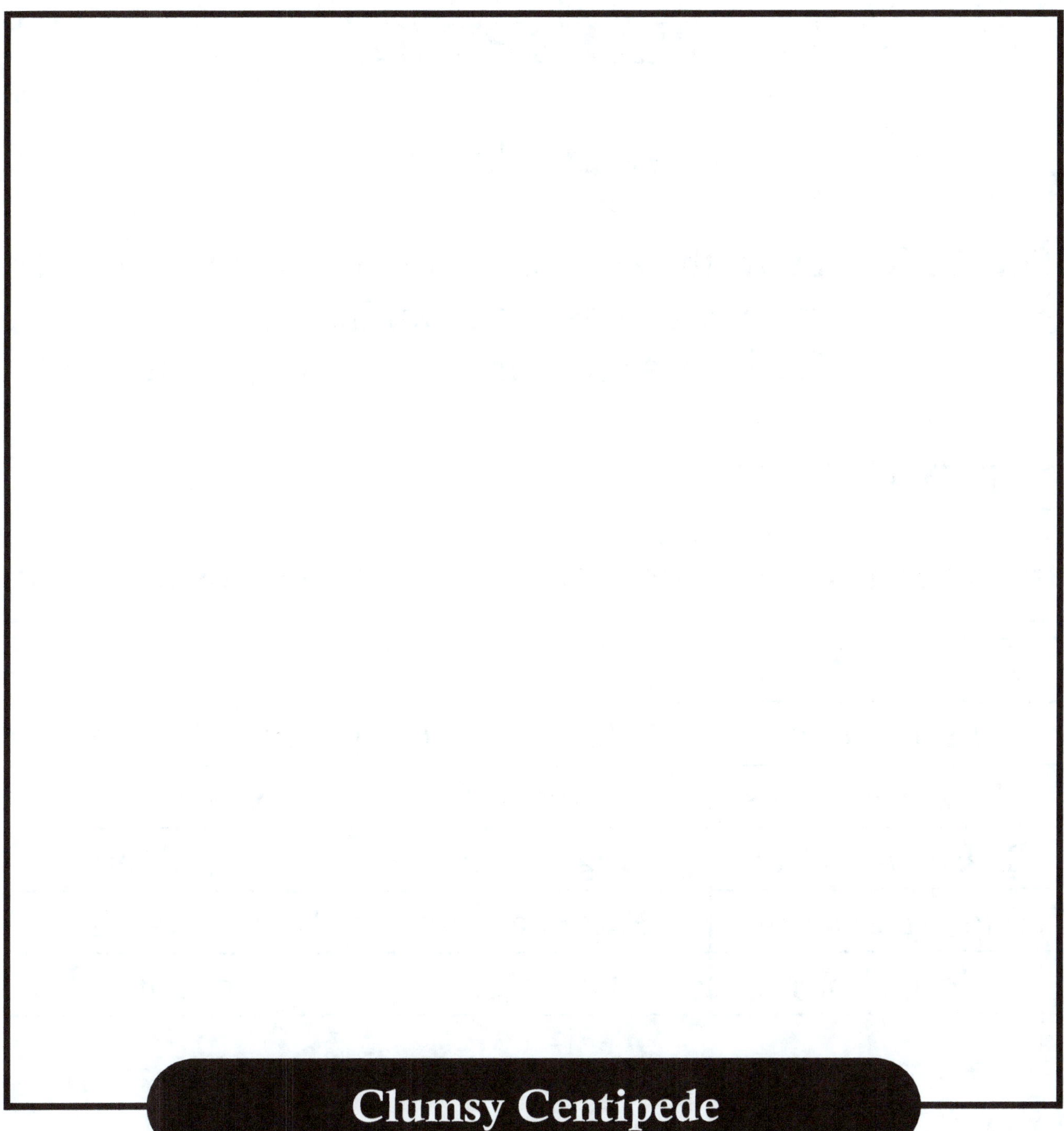

Clumsy Centipede

PROMPT 57

Drunk Deer

The Task: Draw the kind of deer that gets so wasted it routinely finds itself waking up with strange Christmas lawn ornaments lying next to it.

Required Objects:

Incorporate at least three of the following items into your drawing.

Beer Bottles	Whiskey Flask	Santa's Sleigh
Christmas Lights	Handcuffs	Sunglasses
Plastic Reindeer	Piggy Bank	Boxer Shorts
New Year's Hat	Party Favours	Breathalyser Test
Beer Cooler	Police Car	Condoms

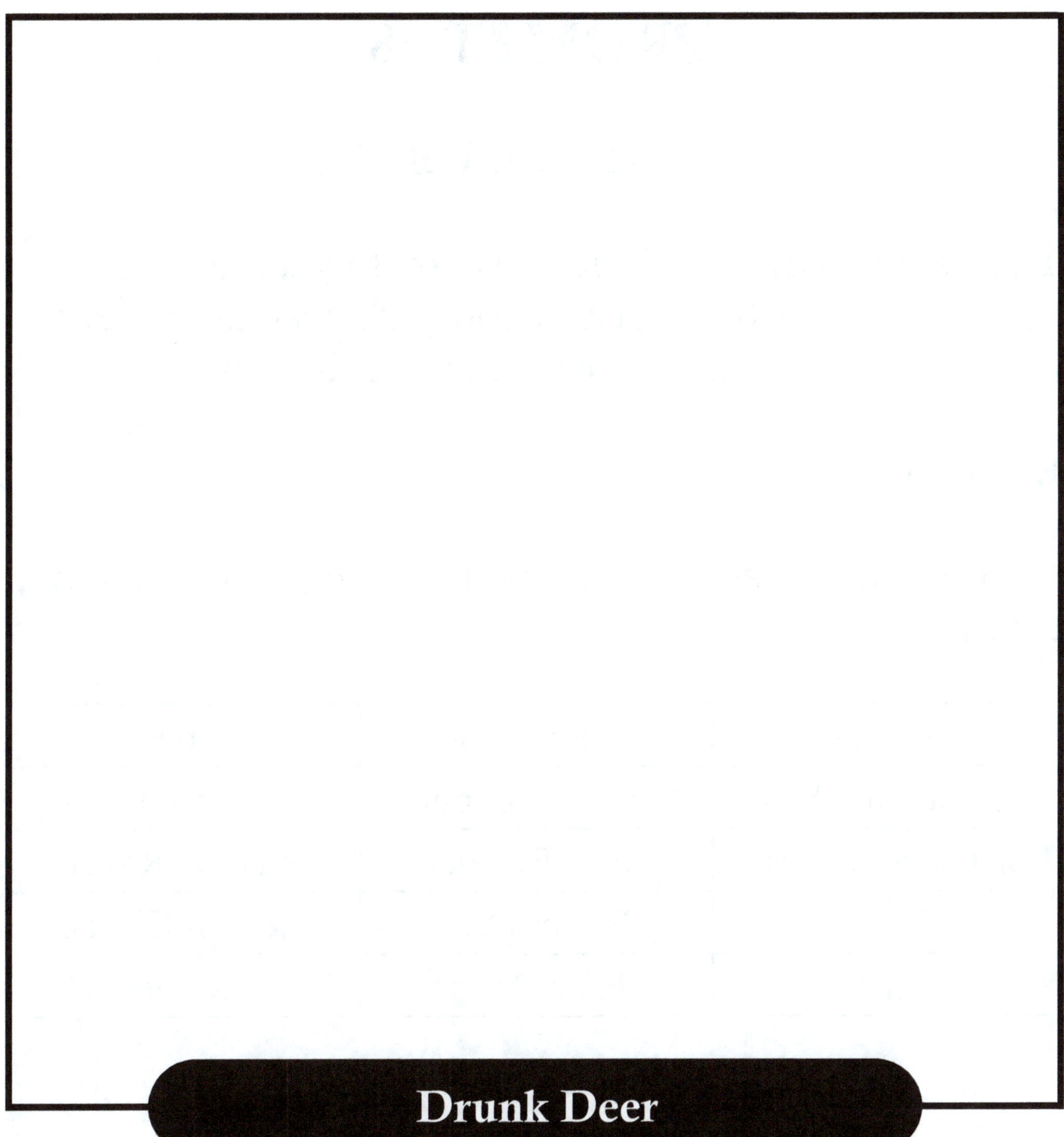

Drunk Deer

PROMPT 58

Efficient Eel

The Task: Draw the kind of eel that would use its electric shock to power its head lamp, iPod as well as other electronic devices.

Required Objects:

Incorporate at least three of the following items into your drawing.

Utility Belt	Battery Cables	Headphones
Oscillating Fan	Laptop Computer	Head Lamp
Rubber Gloves	Juice Blender	Electric Razor
Television	Power Drill	Vacuum Cleaner
Toaster	Hair Dryer	Radio

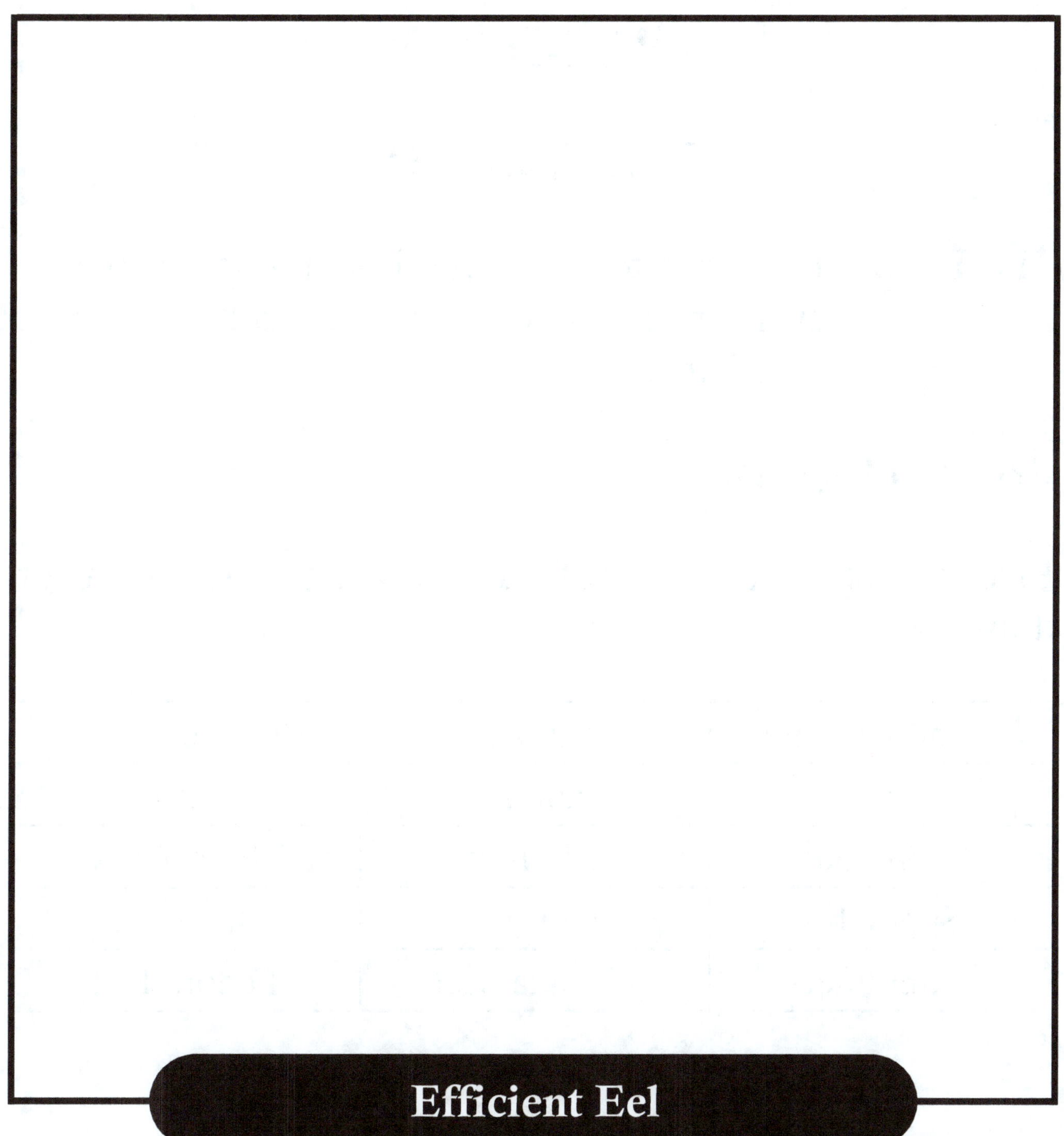

Efficient Eel

PROMPT 59

Cool Caterpillar

The Task: Draw a caterpillar that is so hip is can play every instrument in a jazz quartet all at the same time.

Required Objects:

Incorporate at least three of the following items into your drawing.

Stand Up Bass	Drum Set	Electric Guitar
Piano	Saxophone	Trumpet
Trombone	Clarinet	Microphone
Spotlights	Curtain	Black Tie
Amplifier	Sunglasses	Fedora Hat

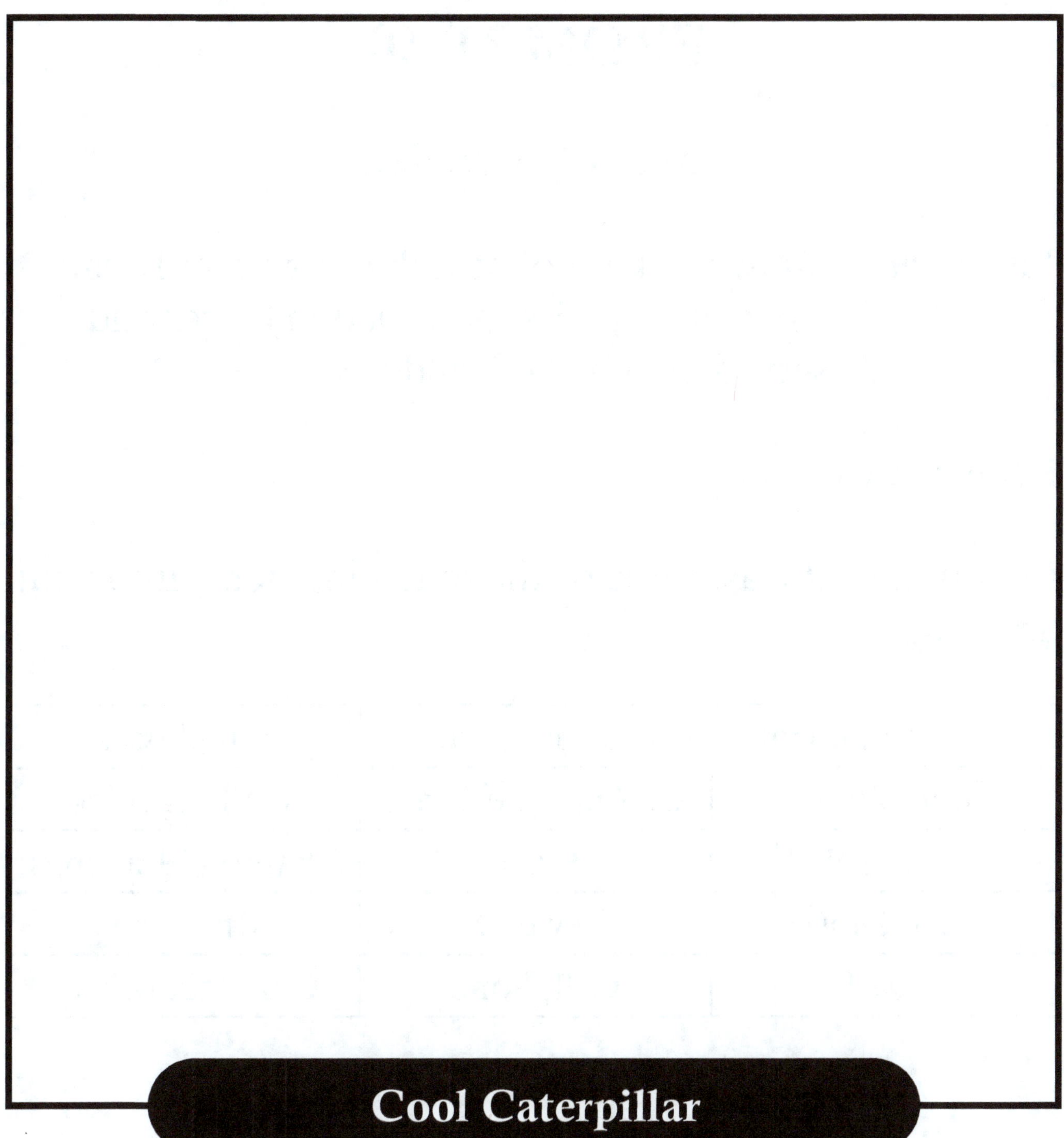

Cool Caterpillar

PROMPT 60

Sophisticated Seal

The Task: Draw the kind of seal that would only eat a fish if it were first pan fried in butter and served on a bed of wild rice.

Required Objects:

Incorporate at least three of the following items into your drawing.

Ladies Sun Hat	Pearl Necklace	Sunglasses
Fur Wrap	Champagne Glass	Walking Stick
Parasol	Purse	Diamond Earrings
Long Gloves	Jewelry	Rickshaw
Scarf	Cellphone	Compact Mirror

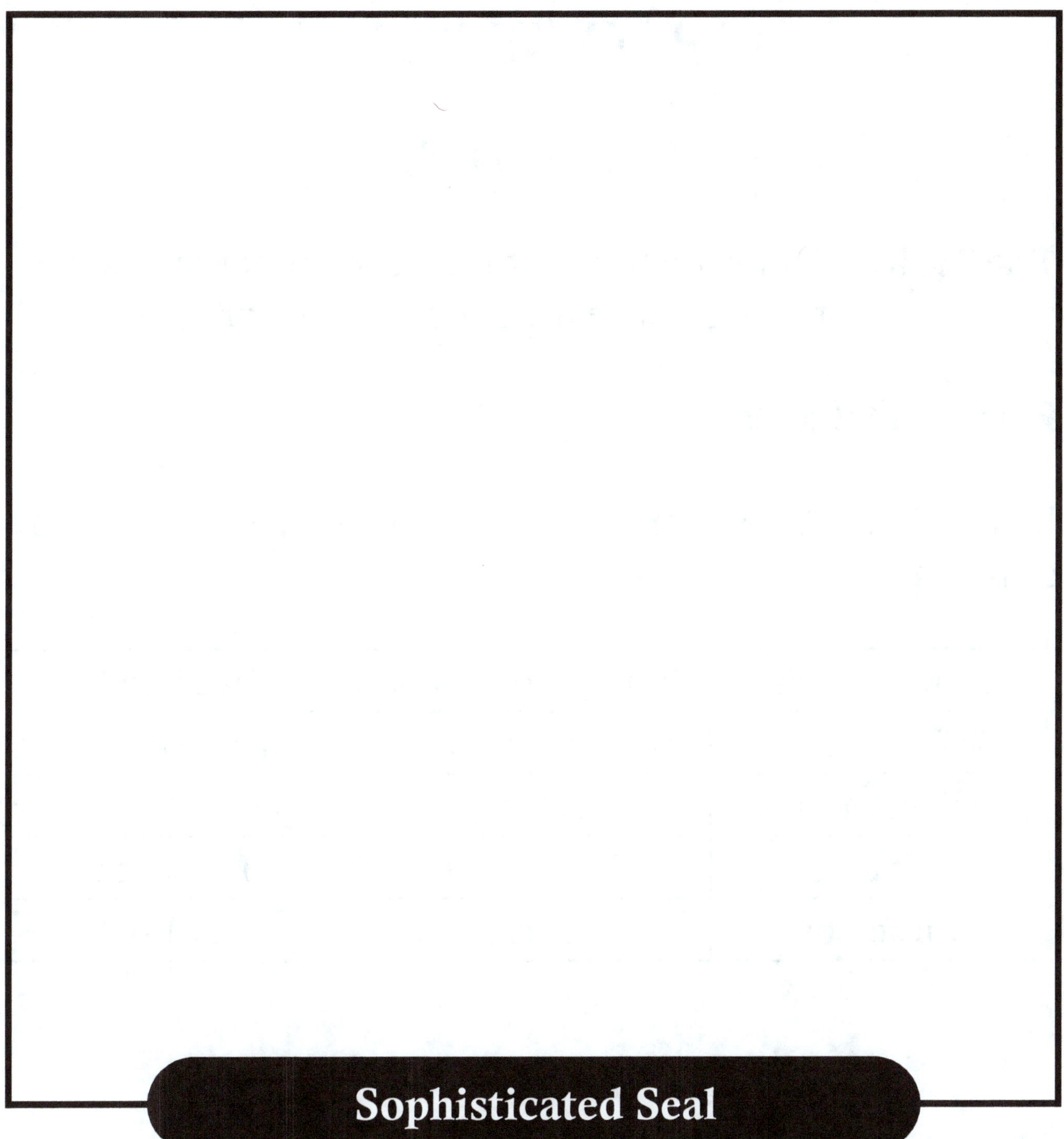
Sophisticated Seal

PROMPT 61

Drowsy Dodo

The Task: Draw a dodo that is so tired it actually slept through the extinction of its entire species.

Required Objects:

Incorporate at least three of the following items into your drawing.

Alarm Clock	Empty Coffee Pot	Saliva Puddle
NyQuil Bottle	Neck Pillow	Fuzzy Slippers
Night Mask	Nightcap	Crescent Moon
Stars	Bird's Nest	Hammock
Music Box	Letter Z	Story Book

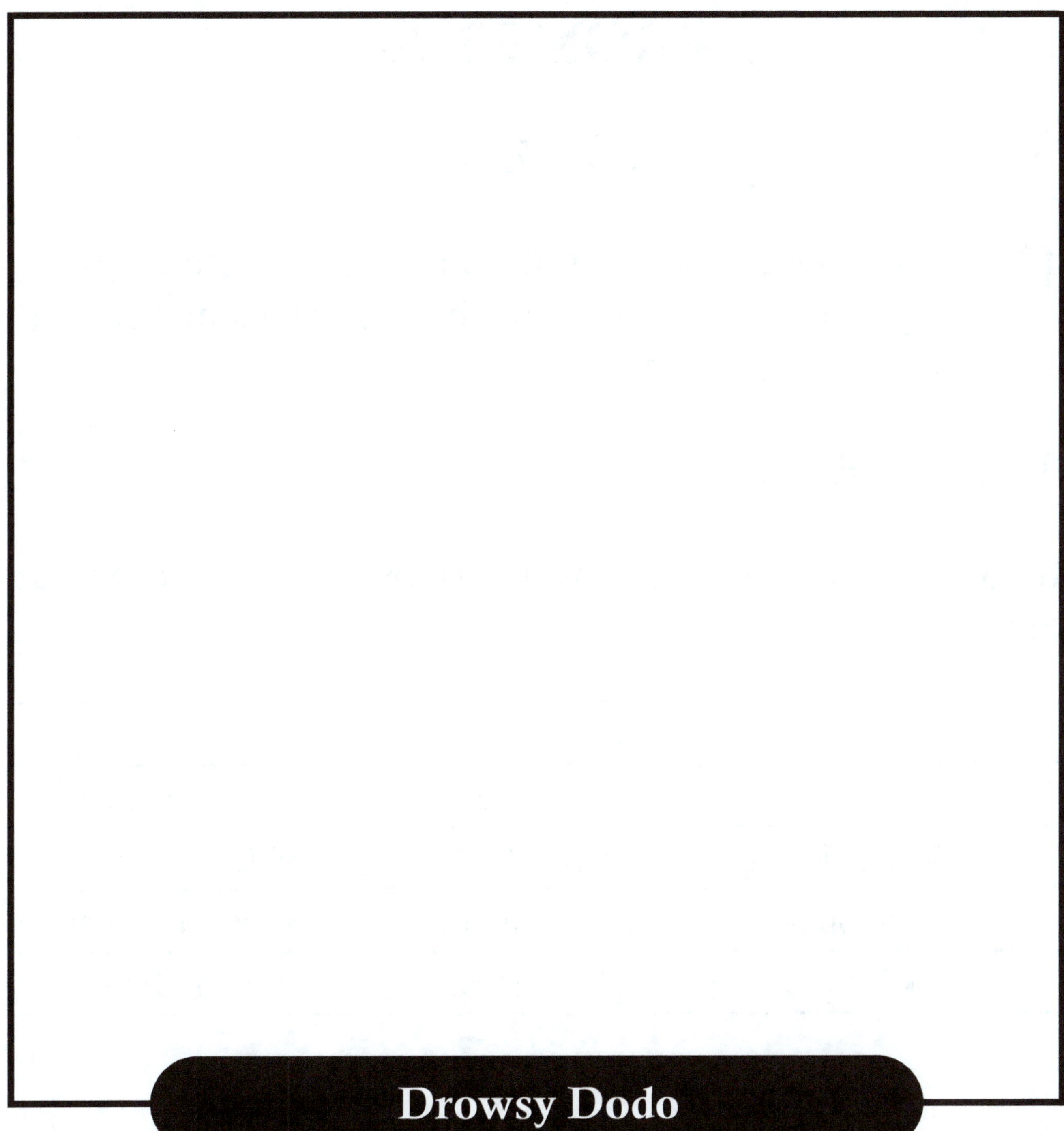
Drowsy Dodo

PROMPT 62

Emo Emu

The Task: Draw the kind of emu that is riddled with teen angst, dyes its feathers black and listens to Goth music.

Required Objects:

Incorporate at least three of the following items into your drawing.

Rain Clouds	Dead Flowers	Black Clothing
Black Wig	Edgar A. Poe Book	Black Lipstick
Spiked Wristbands	Leather Jacket	Military Boots
Headphones	Black Sunglasses	Body Piercings
Black Toque	Headstone	Open Grave

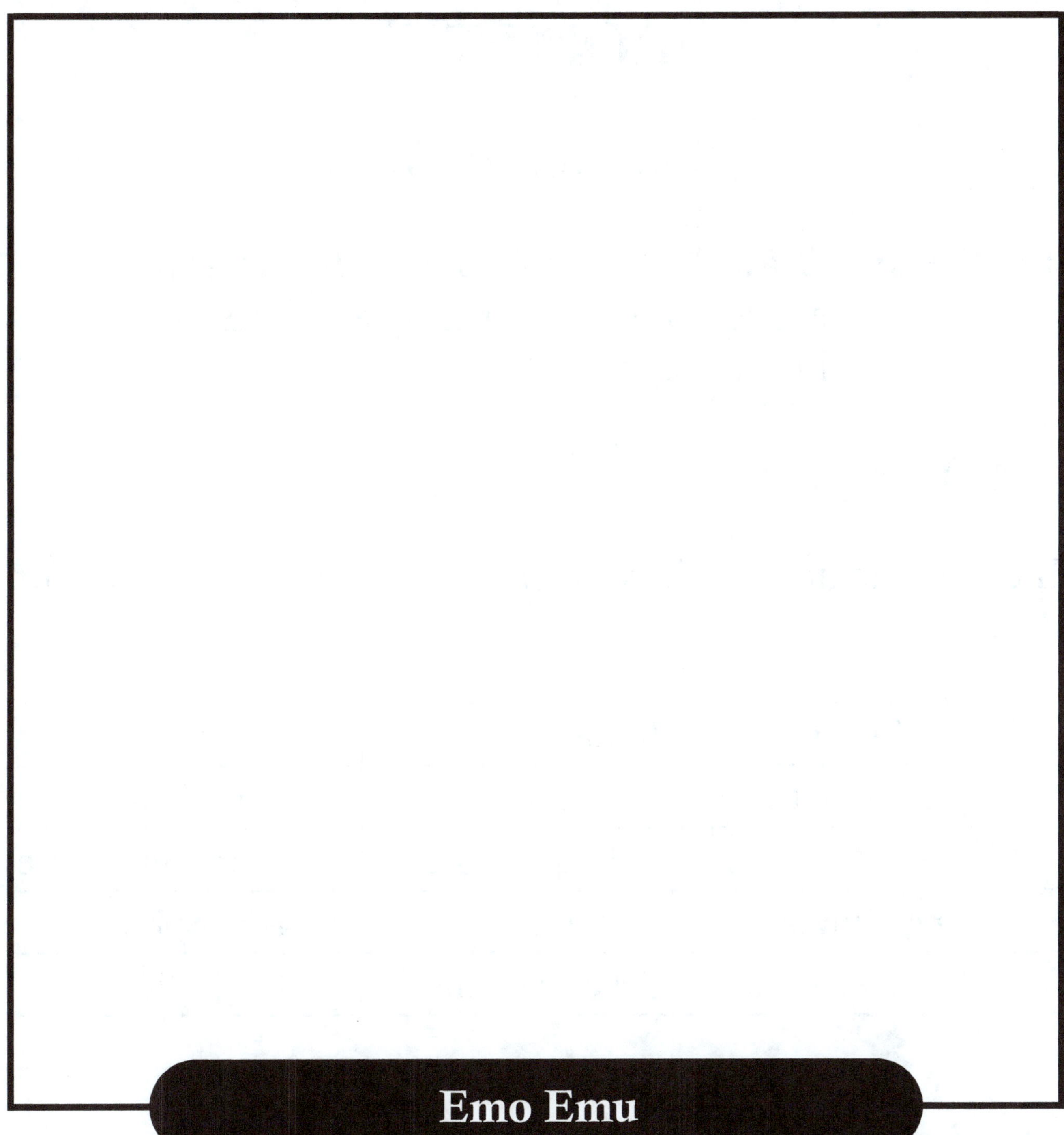

Emo Emu

PROMPT 63

Dazzling Donkey

The Task: Draw the kind of donkey that you would expect to see performing as a showgirl in Las Vegas.

Required Objects:

Incorporate at least three of the following items into your drawing.

Head Dress	Hooped Earrings	Feather Boa
Sequence Outfit	Curtain	Spotlights
High Heel Shoes	Marque Sign	Audience Silhouette
Long Gloves	Balloons	Microphone
Brass Pole	Fake Eyelashes	Lipstick

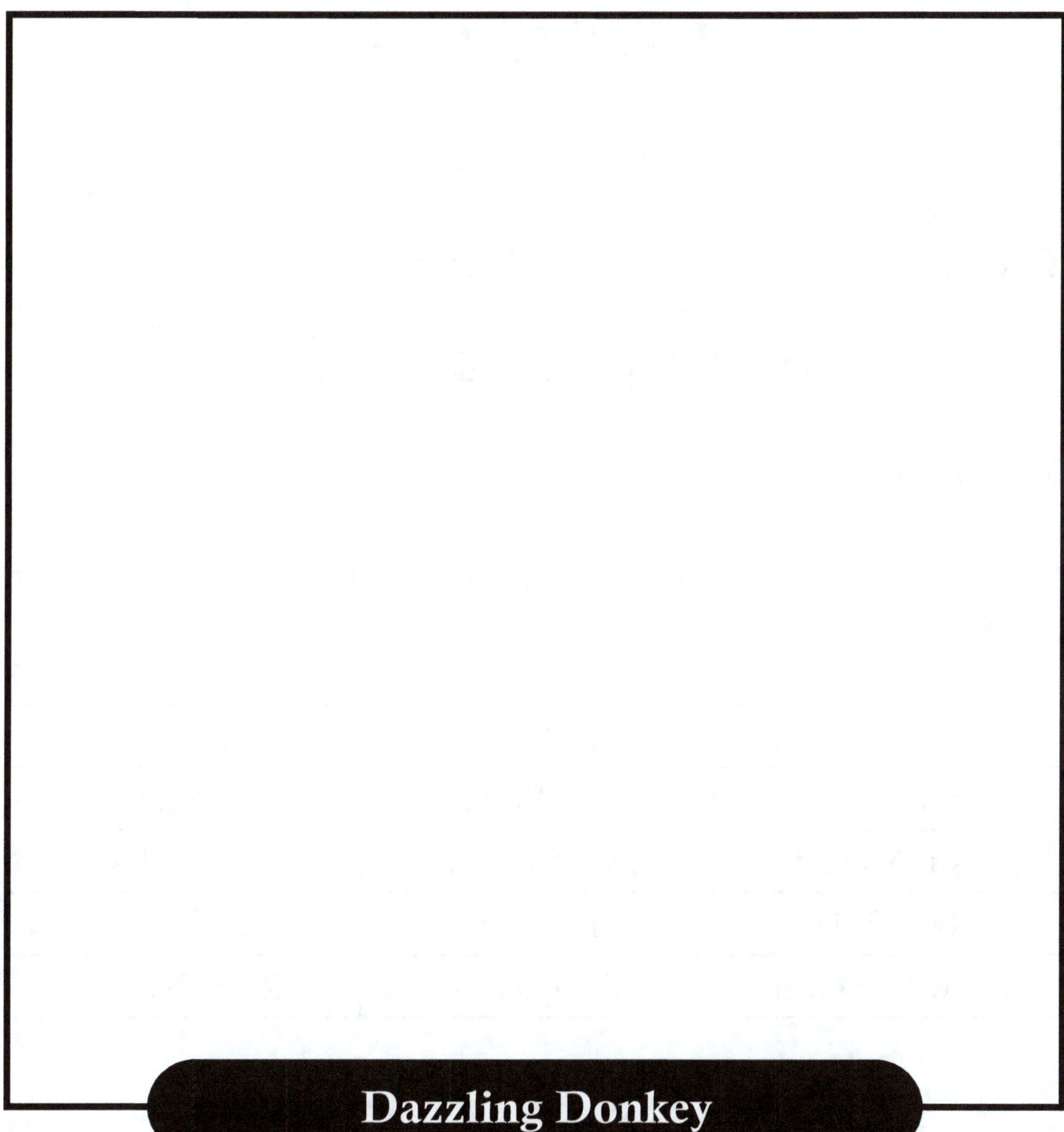

Dazzling Donkey

PROMPT 64

Chatty Cow

The Task: Draw a cow that is so annoyingly talkative, all of the cattle in the near by milking pens actually beg to be taken to the butcher.

Required Objects:

Incorporate at least three of the following items into your drawing.

Headset Phone	Hair Rollers	Mumu Dress
Meat Hook	Ear Plugs	Shotgun
Gossip Magazine	Milking Pen	Salon Chair
Nail File	Tea Cup	Plate of Cookies
Cow Skeleton	Eyeglasses	Rope Noose

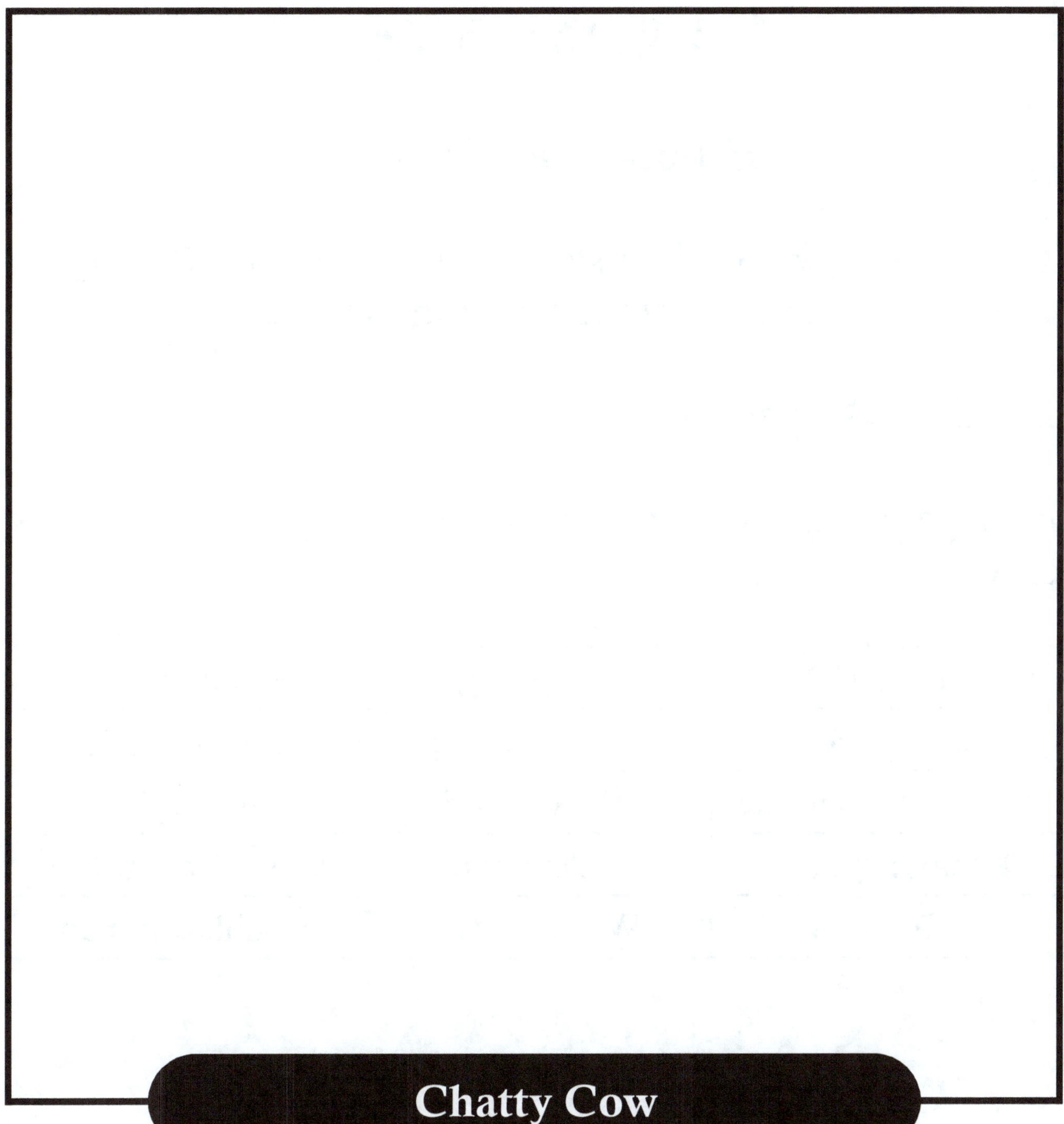

Chatty Cow

PROMPT 65

Humongous Hamster

The Task: Draw a hamster that is so large it can only fit one leg into the running wheel.

Required Objects:

Incorporate at least three of the following items into your drawing.

Undersized T-shirt	Chip Bag	Cookie Box
Candy Bar	Chicken Leg	Hamster Wheel
Big Gulp Container	Head Band	Sweat Suit
Reclining Chair	Television	Whip Cream Can
Donuts	Weight Scale	Oscillating Fan

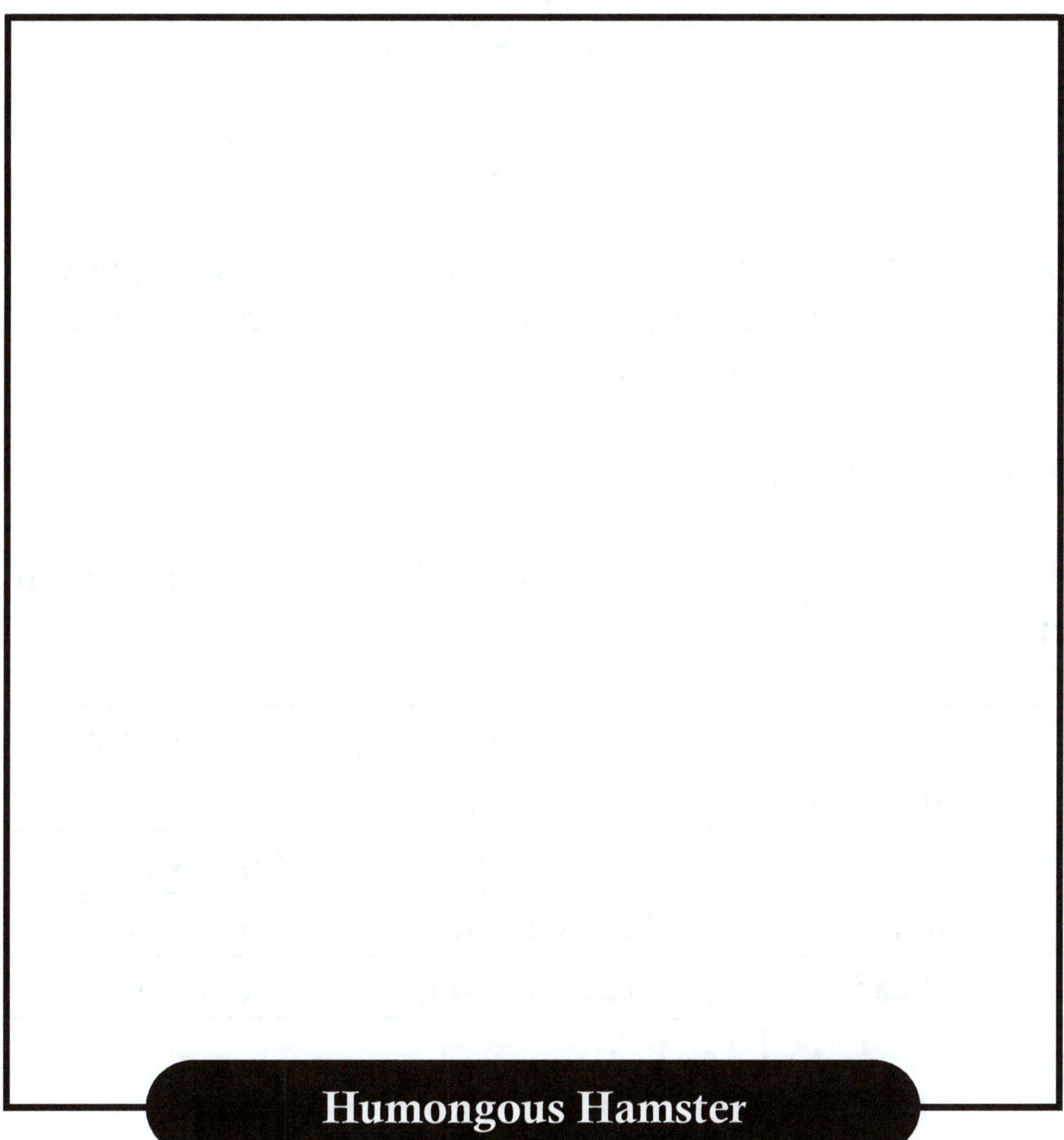

Humongous Hamster

PROMPT 66

Crafty Crab

The Task: Draw the kind of crab that is no stranger to a bedazzling gun or to decorating its shell for the holidays.

Required Objects:

Incorporate at least three of the following items into your drawing.

Bedazzle Gun	Glue Bottle	Paint Brush
Paint Cans	Yarn Ball	Ribbon
Buttons	Scissors	Magic Markers
Glitter Jar	Popsicle Sticks	Crayons
Beads	Jean Clothing	Balloons

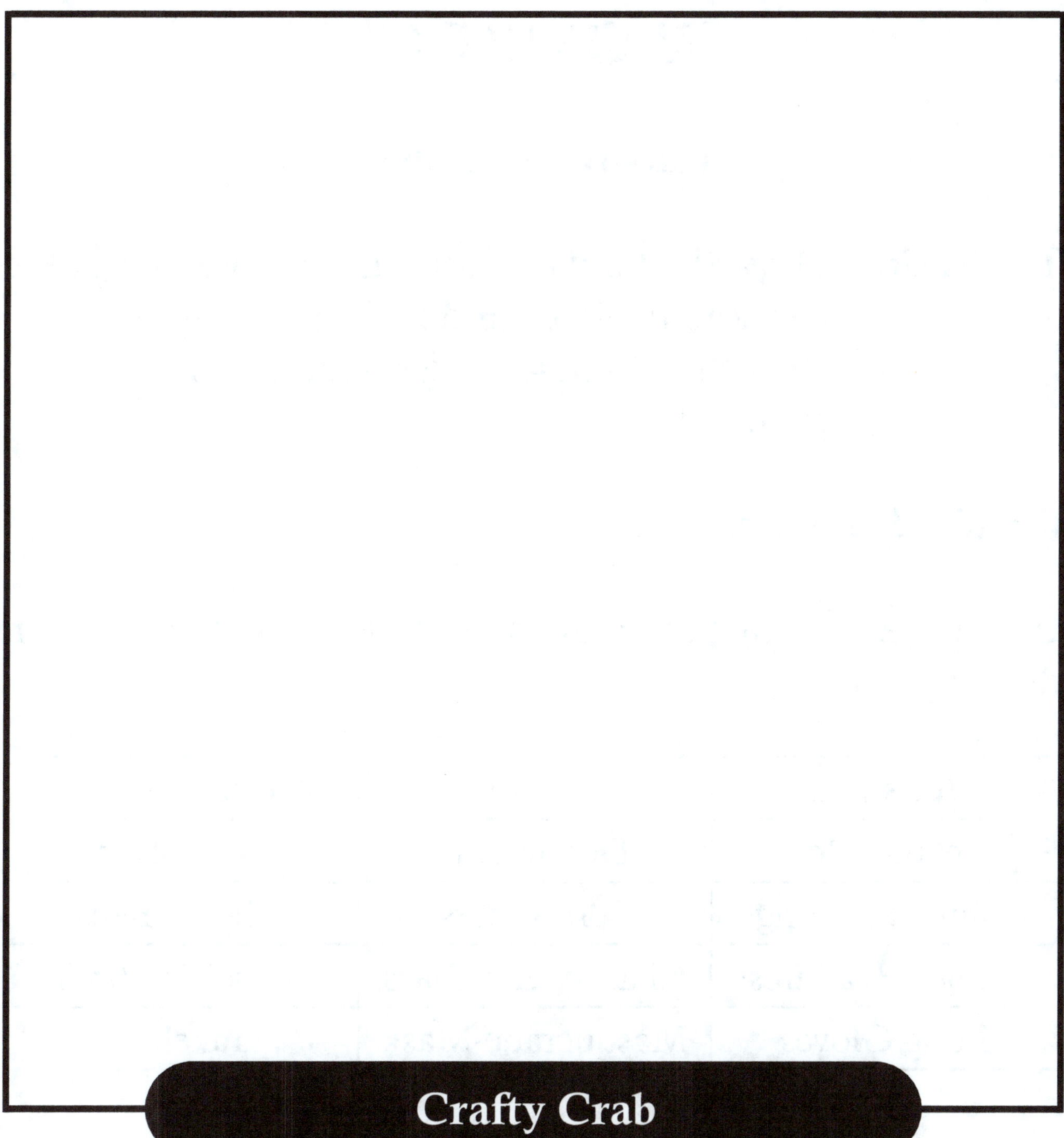

Crafty Crab

PROMPT 67

Flashy Flamingo

The Task: Draw the kind of flamingo that you would be more likely to find making it rain in a strip club, than getting rained on in the everglades.

Required Objects:

Incorporate at least three of the following items into your drawing.

Brass Pole	Bustier	Bunny Ears
Feather Boa	Dollar Bills	Stiletto Heels
Fishnet Stockings	Spot Lights	Garter Belt
Feather Headdress	Champagne Glass	Parasol Umbrella
Long Gloves	Masquerade Mask	Jukebox

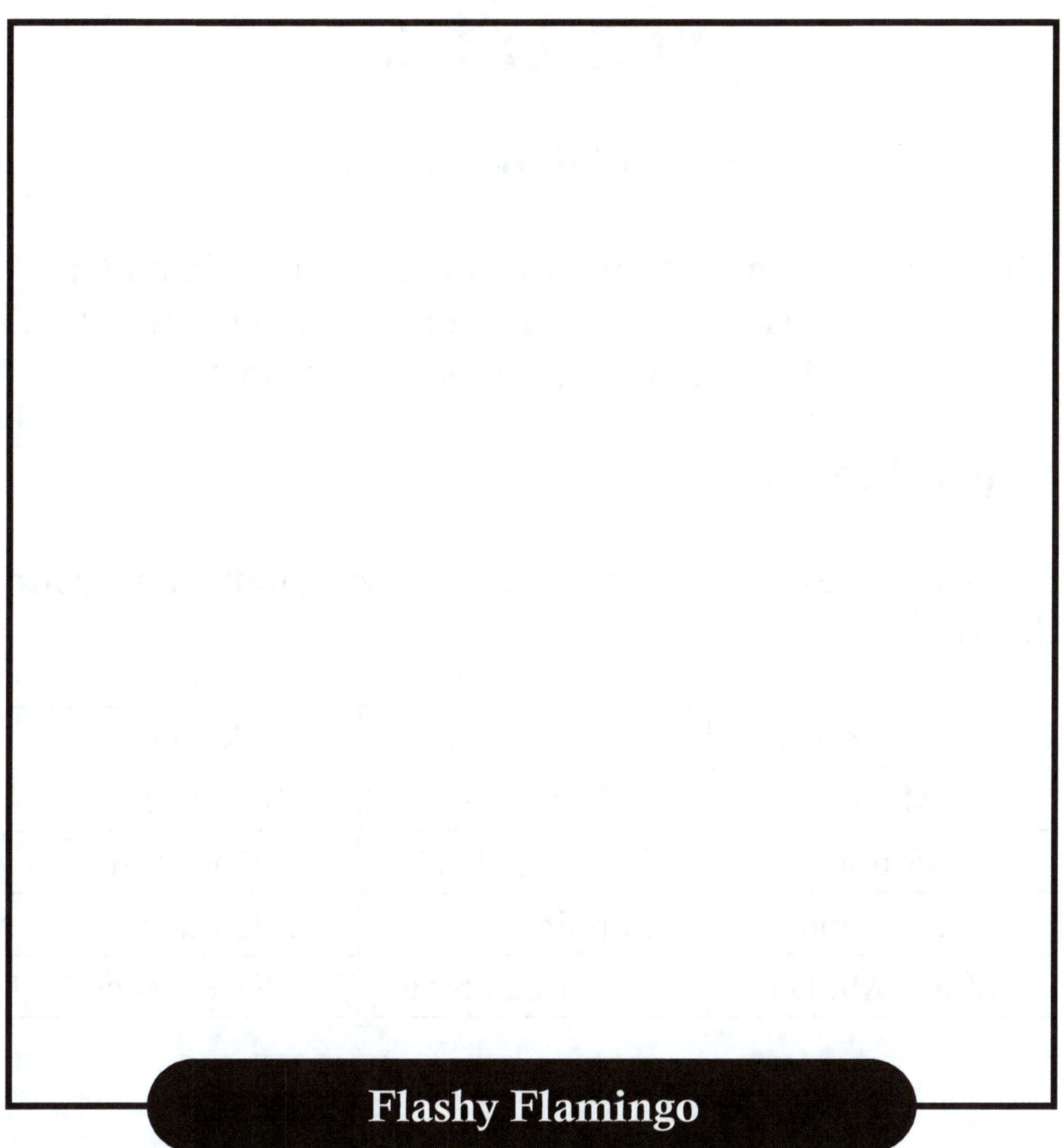

Flashy Flamingo

PROMPT 68

Hurtful Hippopotamus

The Task: Draw the kind of hippopotamus that after losing a few pounds proceeds to point out all of the other hippo's weight problems.

Required Objects:

Incorporate at least three of the following items into your drawing.

Measuring Tape	Weight Scale	Muzzle
Mirror	Diet Pills	Skin Caliper
Girdle	Broccoli Head	Track Suit
Headband	Running Shoes	Pointing Stick
Magic Marker	Wide Load Sign	Rice Cakes

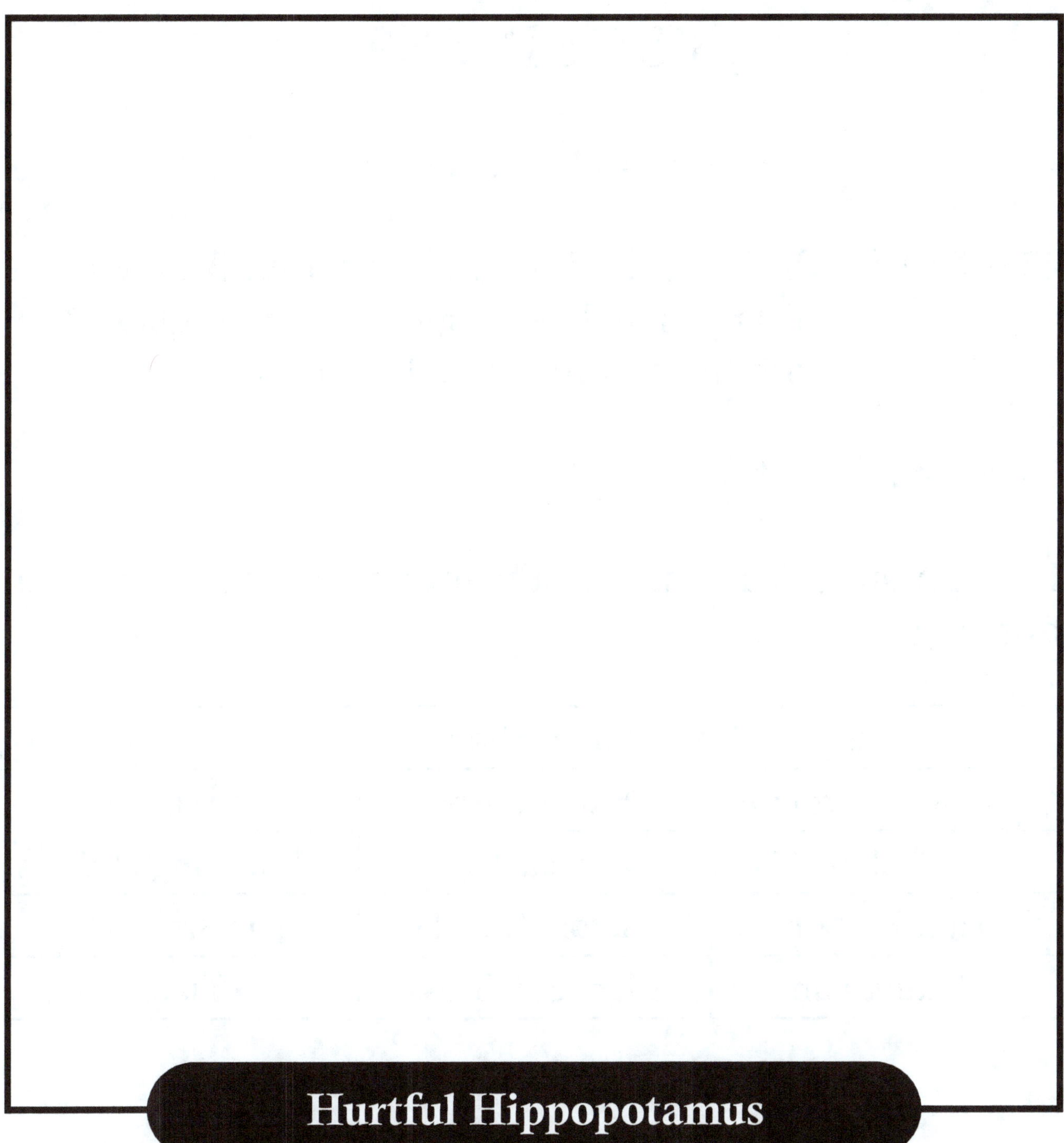

Hurtful Hippopotamus

PROMPT 69

Graceful Giraffe

The Task: Draw the kind of giraffe that unlike the rest of its gangly legged species, actual glides with the elegance of a ballerina.

Required Objects:

Incorporate at least three of the following items into your drawing.

Tutu	Ballet Shoes	Long Gloves
Feather Hairpiece	Ballet Barre	Leg Warmers
Bushes	Acacia Tree	Watering Hole
Hair Ribbon	Victor Victrola	Theatre Seats
Setting Sun	Elephant Grass	Tiara

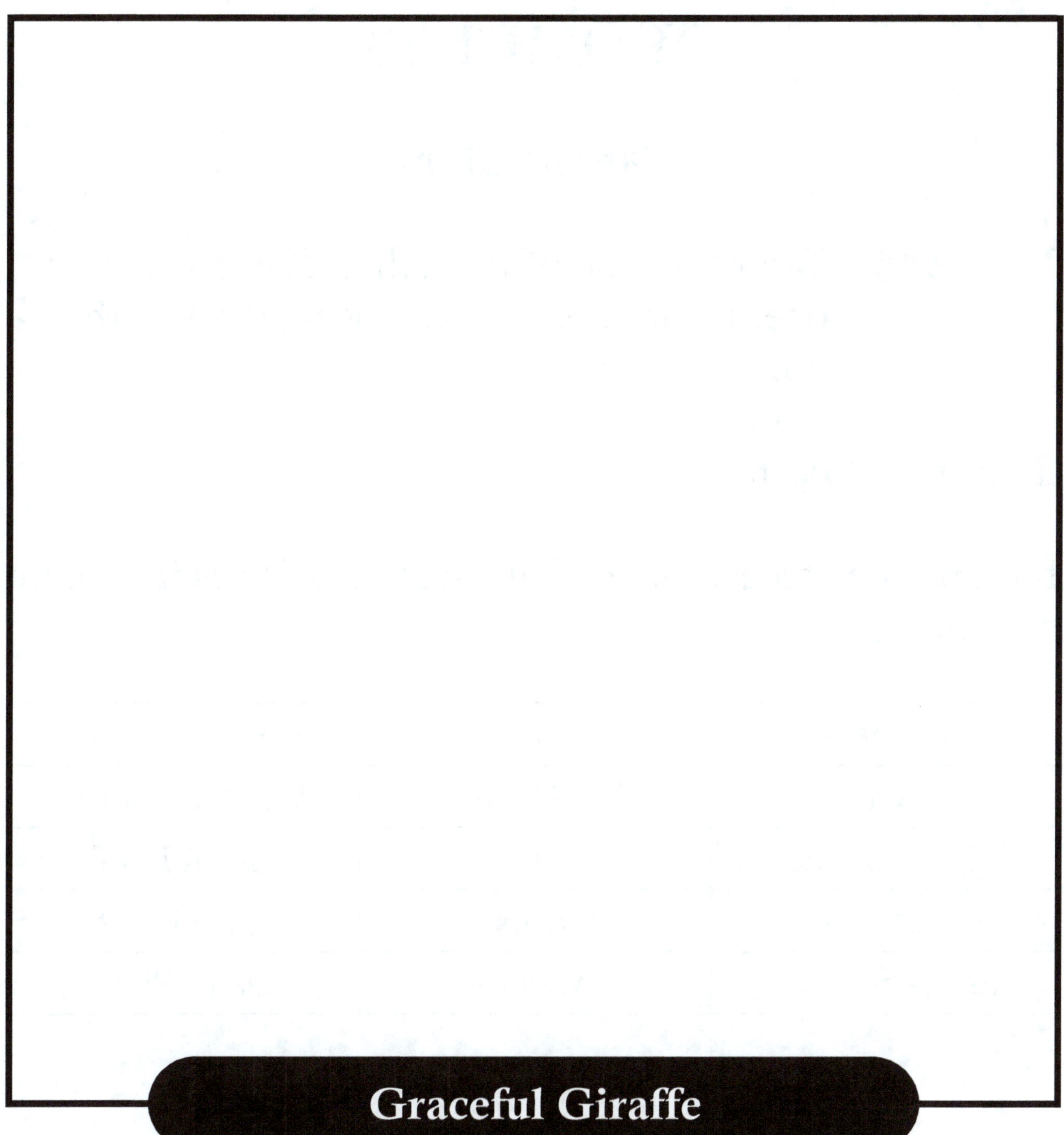

Graceful Giraffe

PROMPT 70

Candid Clam

The Task: Draw the kind of clam that takes pleasure in opening its shell and exposing itself to the other sea life.

Required Objects:

Incorporate at least three of the following items into your drawing.

Camera	Trench Coat	Censored Sign
Pearl	Sun Glasses	Whiskey Bottle
Fedora Hat	Seaweed	Coral Reef
Bubbles	Starfish	Kelp Plant
Sea Anemone	Anchor	Jelly Fish

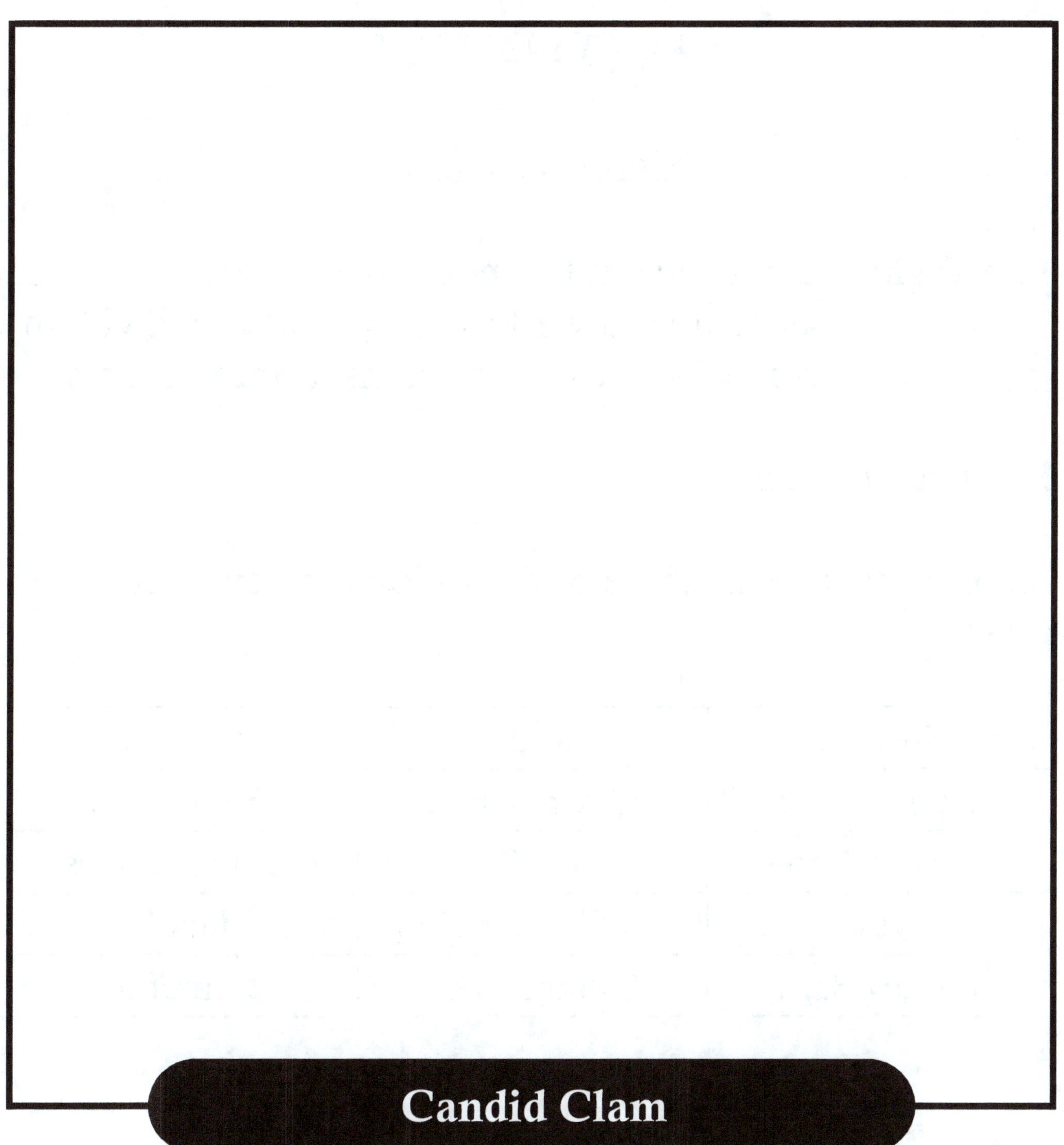

Candid Clam

PROMPT 71

Heinous Horse

The Task: Draw the kind of horse you would expect to see in an old western movie playing a villain who just loves to put damsels into distress.

Required Objects:

Incorporate at least three of the following items into your drawing.

Mustache	Rope	Dynamite
Gun Holster	Cowboy Hat	Train Track
Cowboy Boots	Bolo Tie	Leather Chaps
Vest	Six Shooter Gun	Neck Handkerchief
Money Bags	Saloon Door	Campfire

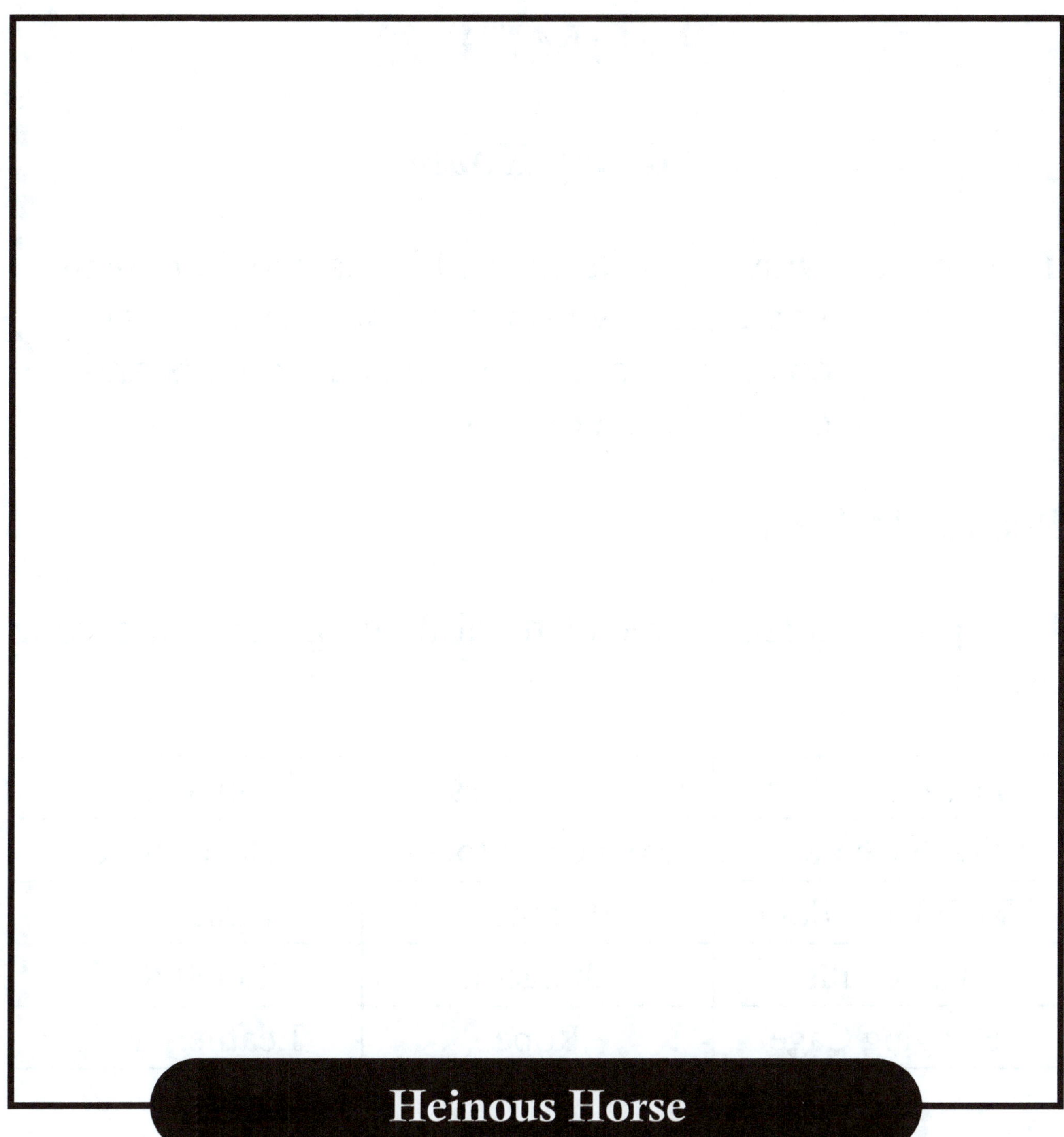

Heinous Horse

PROMPT 72

Kinky Koala

The Task: Draw a koala that unlike its cuddly cousin Paddington who wore a yellow latex rain coat, prefers to don black latex boots and carry a leather whip.

Required Objects:

Incorporate at least three of the following items into your drawing.

Leather Collar	Sunglasses	Blindfold
Wall Chains	Medieval Stocks	Black Hood
Thigh High Boots	Feather	Candles
Handcuffs	Dungeon	Stretch Rack
Hanging Cage	Rope	Leather Whip

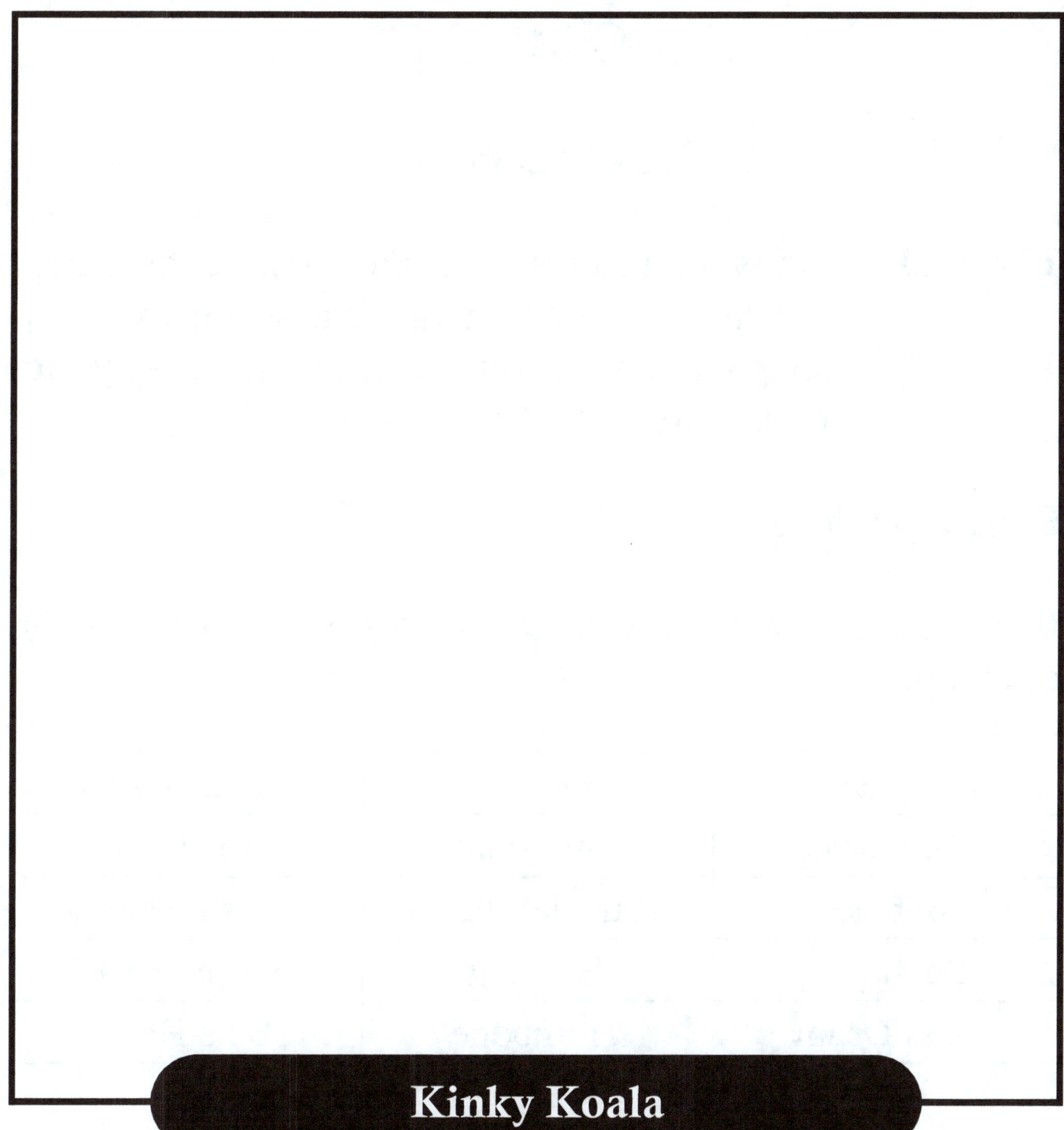

Kinky Koala

PROMPT 73

Lively Lobster

The Task: Draw a lobster that unlike most of the other crustaceans, is so energetic it performs a song and dance routine as diners pass by the tank at the local Surf and Turf.

Required Objects:

Incorporate at least three of the following items into your drawing.

Top Hat	Bow Tie	Walking Stick
Monocle	Aquarium	Air Pump
Bubbles	Artificial Plants	Treasure Chest
Spotlights	Menu Sign	Velvet Rope
Bass Drum	Trombone	Bike Horn

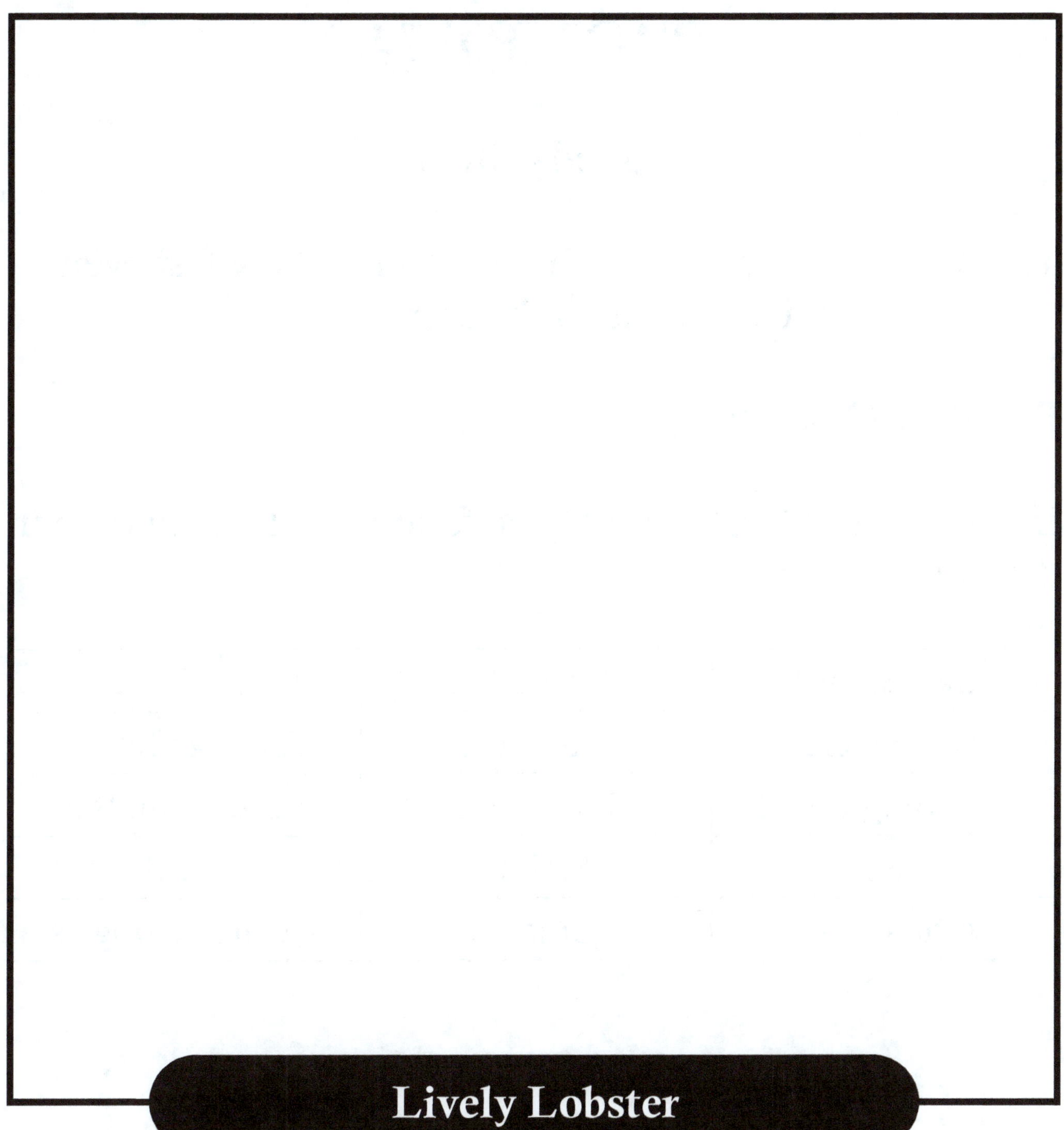

Lively Lobster

PROMPT 74

Speedy Sloth

The Task: Draw a sloth that is so incredibly fast even the cheetahs can't catch it.

Required Objects:

Incorporate at least three of the following items into your drawing.

Skateboard	Electric Fan	Go Kart
Racing Helmet	Scarf	Racing Gloves
Speeding Bullet	Radar Gun	Speed Limit Sign
Missile	Saddle	Speed Boat
Aviator Hat	Smoke	Aviator Googles

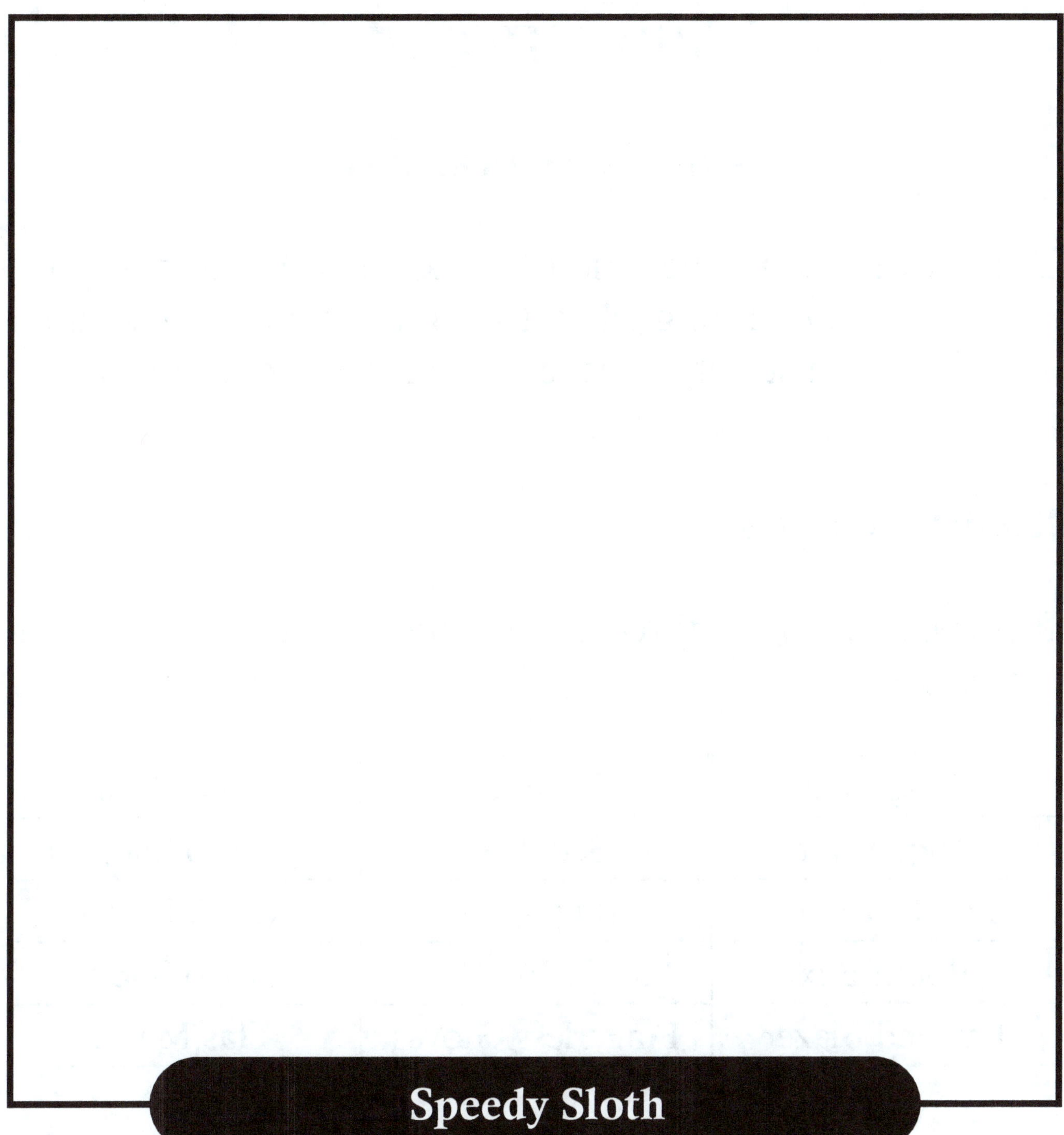

Speedy Sloth

PROMPT 75

Carefree Cockroach

The Task: Draw the kind of cockroach that instead of scattering when the lights come on, instead just puts on its sunglasses and continues on its merry way.

Required Objects:

Incorporate at least three of the following items into your drawing.

Sunglasses	Cigarette	Leather Jacket
Toque Hat	Beer Can	High Top Sneakers
Food Crumbs	Bug Spray	Roach Motel
Boom Box	Pompadour Hair	Hobo Stick
Patched Blazer	Fingerless Gloves	Gas Mask

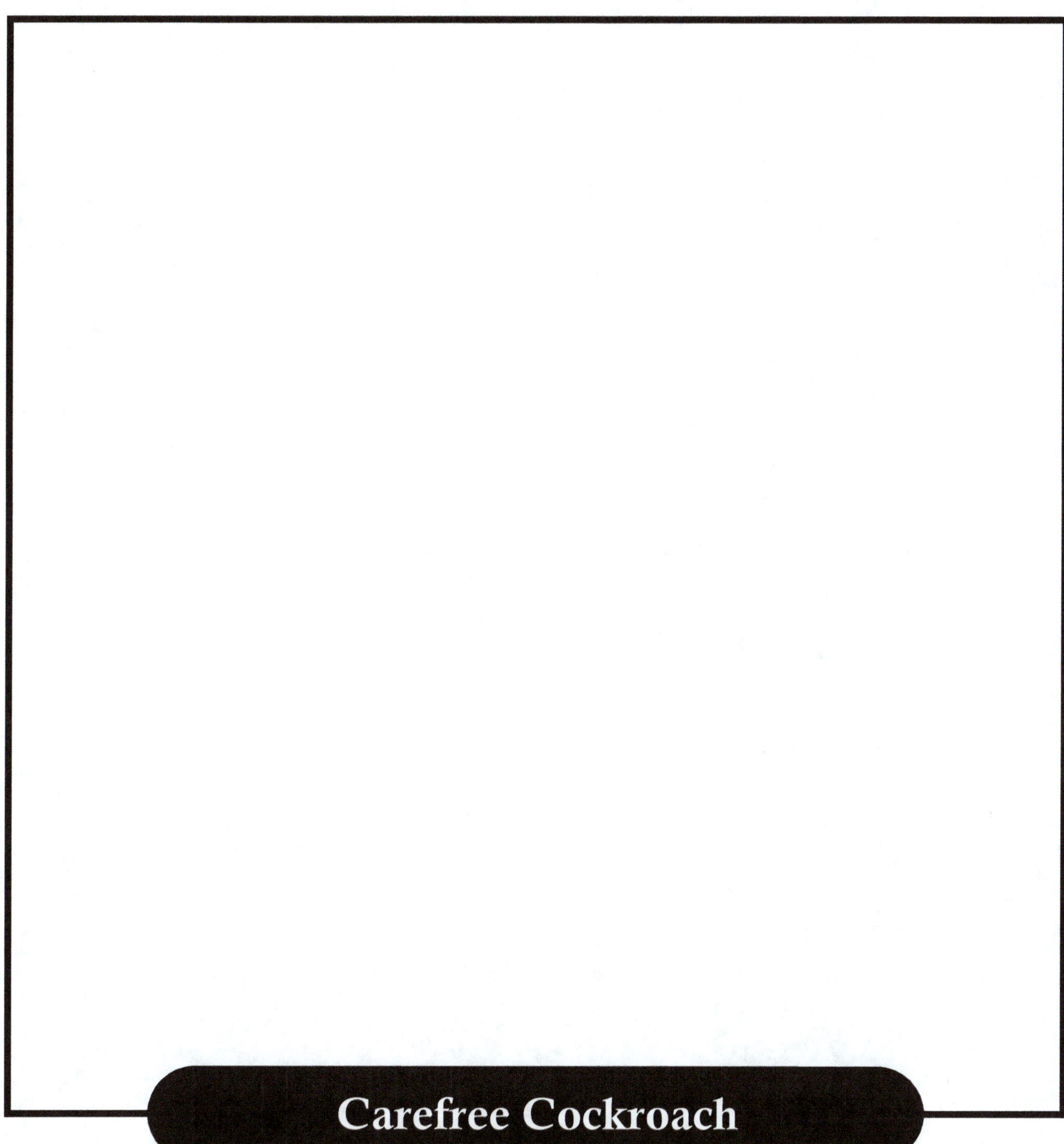

Carefree Cockroach